Chapter 1 - 8085

Architecture

8085 is pronounced as "eighty-eighty-five" microprocessor. It is an 8-bit microprocessor designed by Intel in 1977 using NMOS technology.

It has the following configuration –

- 8-bit data bus
- 16-bit address bus, which can address up to 64KB
- A 16-bit program counter
- A 16-bit stack pointer
- Six 8-bit registers arranged in pairs: BC, DE, HL
- Requires +5V supply to operate at 3.2 MHZ single phase clock

It is used in washing machines, microwave ovens, mobile phones, etc.

Functional Units

8085 consists of the following functional units –

Accumulator

It is an 8-bit register used to perform arithmetic, logical, I/O & LOAD/STORE operations. It is connected to internal data bus & ALU.

Arithmetic and logic unit

As the name suggests, it performs arithmetic and logical operations like Addition, Subtraction, AND, OR, etc. on 8-bit data.

General purpose register

There are 6 general purpose registers in 8085 processor, i.e. B, C, D, E, H & L. Each register can hold 8-bit data.

These registers can work in pair to hold 16-bit data and their pairing combination is like B-C, D-E & H-L.

Program counter

It is a 16-bit register used to store the memory address location of the next instruction to be executed. Microprocessor increments the program whenever an instruction is being executed, so that the program counter points to the memory address of the next instruction that is going to be executed.

Stack pointer

It is also a 16-bit register works like stack, which is always incremented/decremented by 2 during push & pop operations.

Temporary register

It is an 8-bit register, which holds the temporary data of arithmetic and logical operations.

Flag register

It is an 8-bit register having five 1-bit flip-flops, which holds either 0 or 1 depending upon the result stored in the accumulator.

These are the set of 5 flip-flops –
- Sign (S)

- Zero (Z)
- Auxiliary Carry (AC)
- Parity (P)
- Carry (C)

Its bit position is shown in the following table –

D7	D6	D5	D4	D3	D2	D1	D0
S	Z		AC		P		CY

Instruction register and decoder

It is an 8-bit register. When an instruction is fetched from memory then it is stored in the Instruction register. Instruction decoder decodes the information present in the Instruction register.

Timing and control unit

It provides timing and control signal to the microprocessor to perform operations. Following are the timing and control signals, which control external and internal circuits –

- Control Signals: READY, RD', WR', ALE
- Status Signals: So, S1, IO/M'
- DMA Signals: HOLD, HLDA
- RESET Signals: RESET IN, RESET OUT

Interrupt control

As the name suggests it controls the interrupts during a process. When a microprocessor is executing a main program and whenever an interrupt occurs, the microprocessor shifts the control from the main program to process the incoming request. After the request is completed, the control goes back to the main program.

There are 5 interrupt signals in 8085 microprocessor: INTR, RST 7.5, RST 6.5, RST 5.5 and TRAP.

Serial Input/output control

It controls the serial data communication by using these two instructions: SID (Serial input data) and SOD (Serial output data).

Address buffer and address-data buffer

The content stored in the stack pointer and program counter is loaded into the address buffer and address-data buffer to communicate with the CPU. The memory and I/O chips are connected to these buses; the CPU can exchange the desired data with the memory and I/O chips.

Address bus and data bus

Data bus carries the data to be stored. It is bidirectional, whereas address bus carries the location to where it should be stored and it is unidirectional. It is used to transfer the data & Address I/O devices.

We have tried to depict the architecture of 8085 with this following image –

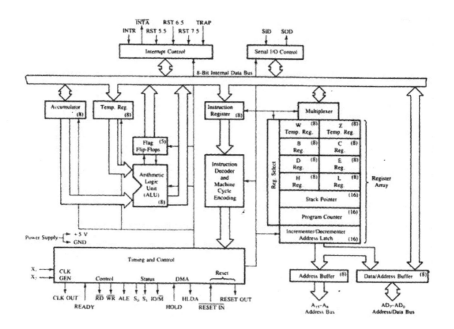

Pin diagram

Pin diagram of 8085 microprocessor is as given below:

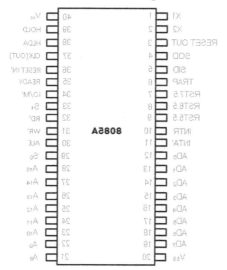

The address bus is a group of sixteen lines i.e A0-A15. The address bus is unidirectional, i.e., bits flow in one direction from the microprocessor unit to the peripheral devices and uses the high order address bus.

Control and Status Signals

- ALE – It is an Address Latch Enable signal. It goes high during first T state of a machine cycle and enables the lower 8-bits of the address, if its value is 1 otherwise data bus is activated.
- IO/M' – It is a status signal which determines whether the address is for input-output or memory. When it is high (1) the address on the address bus is for input-output devices. When it is low (0) the address on the address bus is for the memory.
- S0, S1 – These are status signals. They distinguish the various types of operations such as halt, reading and instruction fetching or writing.
- RD' – It is a signal to control READ operation. When it is low the selected memory or input-output device is read.
- WR' – It is a signal to control WRITE operation. When it goes low the data on the data bus is written into the selected memory or I/O location.
- READY – It senses whether a peripheral is ready to transfer data or not. If READY is high (1) the peripheral is ready. If it is low (0) the microprocessor waits till it goes high. It is useful for interfacing low speed devices.

IO/M'	S1	S0	Data Bus Status
0	1	1	Opcode fetch
0	1	0	Memory read
0	0	1	Memory write
1	1	0	I/O read

1	0	1	I/O write
1	1	1	Interrupt acknowledge
0	0	0	Halt

Power Supply and Clock Frequency

- Vcc – +5v power supply
- Vss – Ground Reference
- XI, X2 – A crystal is connected at these two pins. The frequency is internally divided by two, therefore, to operate a system at 3MHZ the crystal should have frequency of 6MHZ.
- CLK (OUT) – This signal can be used as the system clock for other devices.

Interrupts and Peripheral Initiated Signals

8085 has five interrupt signals that can be used to interrupt a program execution.
- INTR
- RST 7.5
- RST 6.5
- RST 5.5
- TRAP

The microprocessor acknowledges Interrupt Request by INTA' signal. In addition to Interrupts, there are three externally initiated signals namely RESET, HOLD and READY. To respond to HOLD request, it has one signal called HLDA.
- INTR – It is an interrupt request signal.
- INTA' – It is an interrupt acknowledgment sent by the microprocessor after INTR is received.

- **RESET IN'** – When the signal on this pin is low (0), the program-counter is set to zero, the buses are tristate and the microprocessor unit is reset.
- **RESET OUT** – This signal indicates that the MPU is being reset. The signal can be used to reset other devices.

DMA Signals

- **HOLD** – It indicates that another device is requesting the use of the address and data bus. Having received HOLD request the microprocessor relinquishes the use of the buses as soon as the current machine cycle is completed. Internal processing may continue. After the removal of the HOLD signal the processor regains the bus.
- **HLDA** – It is a signal which indicates that the hold request has been received after the removal of a HOLD request, the HLDA goes low.

Serial I/O Ports

Serial transmission in 8085 is implemented by the two signals,

- **SID and SOD** – SID is a data line for serial input where as SOD is a data line for serial output.

Registers

A microprocessor is a multipurpose, programmable, clock-driven, register-based electronic device that reads binary instructions from a storage device called memory, accepts binary data as input and processes data according to those instructions and provide results as output. A 8085 microprocessor, is a second generation 8-bit microprocessor and is the base for studying and using all the microprocessor available in the market.

General Purpose Registers

The 8085 has six general-purpose registers to store 8-bit data; these are identified as- B, C, D, E, H, and L. These can be combined as register pairs – BC, DE, and HL, to perform some 16-bit operation.

These registers are used to store or copy temporary data, by using instructions, during the execution of the program.

Accumulator

The Accumulator is an 8-bit register (can store 8-bit data) that is the part of the arithmetic and logical unit (ALU). After performing arithmetical or logical operations, the result is stored in accumulator. Accumulator is also defined as register A.

Flag registers

B_7	B_6	B_5	B_4	B_3	B_2	B_1	B_0
S	Z	---	AC	---	P	---	CY

The flag register is a special purpose register and it is completely different from other registers in microprocessor. It consists of 8 bits and only 5 of them are useful. The other three are left vacant and are used in the future Intel versions. These 5 flags are set or reset (when value of flag is 1, then it is said to be set and when value is 0, then it is said to be reset) after an operation according to data condition of the result in the accumulator and other registers.

The 5 flag registers are:

Sign Flag

It occupies the seventh bit of the flag register, which is also known as
the most significant bit. It helps the programmer to know whether the number stored in the accumulator is positive or negative. If the sign flag is set, it means that number stored in the accumulator is negative, and if reset, then the number is positive.
from 00H to 7F, sign flag is 0
from 80H to FF, sign flag is 1
MSB is 1 (negative)
MSB is 0 (positive)

MVI A 30 (load 30H in register A)
MVI B 40 (load 40H in register B)
SUB B (A = A – B)
These set of instructions will set the sign flag to 1 as 30 – 40 is a negative number.
MVI A 40 (load 40H in register A)
MVI B 30 (load 30H in register B)
SUB B (A = A – B)
These set of instructions will reset the sign flag to 0 as 40 – 30 is a positive number.

Zero Flag

It occupies the sixth bit of the flag register. It is set, when the operation performed in the ALU results in zero (all 8 bits are zero), otherwise it is reset. It helps in determining if two numbers are equal or not.
00H zero flag is 1.
from 01H to FFH zero flag is 0
zero result
0- non-zero result

Example

MVI A 10 (load 10H in register A)
SUB A (A = A – A)
These set of instructions will set the zero flag to 1 as 10H – 10H is 00H

Auxiliary Carry Flag

It occupies the fourth bit of the flag register. In an arithmetic operation, when a carry flag is generated by the third bit and passed on to the fourth bit, then Auxiliary Carry flag is set. If not flag is reset. This flag is used internally for BCD (Binary-Coded decimal Number) operations.

Note: This is the only flag register in 8085 which is not accessible by user.
1-carry out from bit 3 on addition or borrow into bit 3 on subtraction
0-otherwise

MOV A 2B (load 2BH in register A)
MOV B 39 (load 39H in register B)
ADD B (A = A + B)
These set of instructions will set the auxiliary carry flag to 1, as on adding 2B and 39, addition of lower order nibbles B and 9 will generate a carry.

Parity Flag

It occupies the second bit of the flag register. This flag tests for number of 1's in the accumulator. If the accumulator holds even number of 1's, then this flag is set and it is said to even parity. On the other hand if the number of 1's is odd, then it is reset and it is said to be odd parity.

1-accumulator has even number of 1 bits
0-accumulator has odd parity

Example

MVI A 05 (load 05H in register A)
This instruction will set the parity flag to 1 as the BCD code of 05H is 00000101, which contains even number of ones i.e. 2.

Carry Flag

It occupies the zeroth bit of the flag register. If the arithmetic operation results in a carry (if result is more than 8 bit), then Carry Flag is set; otherwise it is reset.

1-carry out from MSB bit on addition or borrow into MSB bit on subtraction
0-no carry out or borrow into MSB bit

Example

MVI A 30 (load 30H in register A)
MVI B 40 (load 40H in register B)
SUB B (A = A – B)
These set of instructions will set the carry flag to 1 as 30 – 40 generates a carry/borrow.
MVI A 40 (load 40H in register A)
MVI B 30 (load 30H in register B)
SUB B (A = A – B)
These set of instructions will reset the sign flag to 0 as 40 – 30 does not generate any carry/borrow.

Memory Registers

There are two 16-bit registers used to hold memory addresses. The size of these registers is 16 bits because the memory addresses are 16 bits. They are:

Program Counter

This register is used to sequence the execution of the instructions. The function of the program counter is to point to the memory address from which the next byte is to be fetched. When a byte (machine code) is being fetched, the program counter is incremented by one to point to the next memory location.

Stack Pointer

It is used as a memory pointer. It points to a memory location in read/write memory, called the stack. It is always incremented/decremented by 2 during push and pop operation.

Here two binary numbers are added. The result produced is stored in the accumulator. Now let's check what each bit means. Refer to the below explanation simultaneously to connect them with the example.

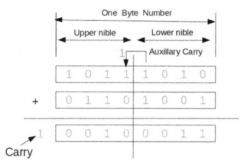

- Sign Flag (7th bit): It is reset (0), which means number stored in the accumulator is positive.
- Zero Flag (6th bit): It is reset (0), thus result of the operations performed in the ALU is non-zero.
- Auxiliary Carry Flag (4th bit): We can see that b3 generates a carry which is taken by b4, thus auxiliary carry flag gets set (1).
- Parity Flag (2nd bit): It is reset (0), it means that parity is odd. The accumulator holds odd number of 1's.
- Carry Flag (0th bit): It is set (1), output results in more than 8 bit.

Addressing Modes

The way of specifying data to be operated by an instruction is called addressing mode.
8085 microprocessor there are 5 types of addressing modes:

Immediate Addressing Mode

In immediate addressing mode the source operand is always data. If the data is 8-bit, then the instruction will be of 2 bytes, if the data is of 16-bit then the instruction will be of 3 bytes.

Example

MVI B 45 (move the data 45H immediately to register B)
LXI H 3050 (load the H-L pair with the operand 3050H immediately)
JMP address (jump to the operand address immediately)

Register Addressing Mode

In register addressing mode, the data to be operated is available inside the register(s) and register(s) is (are) operands. Therefore the operation is performed within various registers of the microprocessor.

Example

MOV A, B (move the contents of register B to register A)
ADD B (add contents of registers A and B and store the result in register A)
INR A (increment the contents of register A by one)

Direct Addressing Mode

In direct addressing mode, the data to be operated is available inside a memory location and that memory location is directly specified as an operand. The operand is directly available in the instruction itself.

LDA 2050 (load the contents of memory location into accumulator A)
LHLD address (load contents of 16-bit memory location into H-L register pair)
IN 35 (read the data from port whose address is 01)

Register Indirect Addressing Mode

IN register indirect addressing mode, the data to be operated is available inside a memory location and that memory location is indirectly specified b a register pair.

Example

MOV A, M (move the contents of the memory location pointed by the H-L pair to the accumulator)
LDAX B (move contains of B-C register to the accumulator)
LXIH 9570 (load immedlate the H-L pair with the address of the location 9570)

Implied/Implicit Addressing Mode

In implied/implicit addressing mode the operand is hidden and the data to be operated is available in the instruction itself.

Example

CMA (finds and stores the 1's complement of the contains of accumulator A in A)
RRC (rotate accumulator A right by one bit)
RLC (rotate accumulator A left by one bit)

Arithmetic Instructions

Arithmetic Instructions are the instructions which perform basic arithmetic operations such as addition, subtraction and a few more. In 8085 microprocessor, the destination operand is generally the accumulator. In 8085 microprocessor, the destination operand is generally the accumulator.

Following is the table showing the list of arithmetic instructions:

Opcode	Operand	Explanation	Example
ADD	R	A = A + R	ADD B
ADD	M	A = A + Mc	ADD 2050
ADI	8-bit data	A = A + 8-bit data	ADD 50
ADC	R	A = A + R + prev. carry	ADC B
ADC	M	A = A + Mc + prev. carry	ADC 2050
ACI	8-bit data	A = A + 8-bit data + prev. carry	ACI 50
SUB	R	A = A − R	SUB B
SUB	M	A = A − Mc	SUB 2050
SUI	8-bit	A = A − 8-	SUI 50

		data	bit data	
SBB	R	A = A – R – prev. carry	SBB B
SBB	M	A = A – Mc -prev. carry	SBB 2050
SBI	8-bit data	A = A – 8- bit data – prev. carry	SBI 50
INR	R	R = R + 1	INR B
INR	M	M = Mc + 1	INR 2050
INX	r.p.	r.p. = r.p. + 1	INX H
DCR	R	R = R – 1	DCR B
DCR	M	M = Mc – 1	DCR 2050
DCX	r.p.	r.p. = r.p. – 1	DCX H
DAD	r.p.	HL = HL + r.p.	DAD H

In the table,
R stands for register
M stands for memory
Mc stands for memory contents
r.p. stands for register pair

Logical Instructions

Logical instructions are the instructions which perform basic logical operations such as AND, OR, etc. In 8085 microprocessor, the destination operand is always the accumulator. Here logical operation works on a bitwise level.

Following is the table showing the list of logical instructions:

Opcode	Operand	Destination	Example
ANA	R	A = A AND R	ANA B
ANA	M	A = A AND Mc	ANA 2050
ANI	8-bit data	A = A AND 8-bit data	ANI 50
ORA	R	A = A OR R	ORA B
ORA	M	A = A OR Mc	ORA 2050
ORI	8-bit data	A = A OR 8-bit data	ORI 50
XRA	R	A = A XOR R	XRA B
XRA	M	A = A XOR Mc	XRA 2050
XRI	8-bit data	A = A XOR 8-bit data	XRI 50
CMA	none	A = 1's compliment of A	CMA
CMP	R	Compares R with A and triggers the flag register	CMP B
CMP	M	Compares Mc with A and triggers the flag register	CMP 2050
CPI	8-bit data	Compares 8-bit data with A and triggers the flag register	CPI 50
RRC	none	Rotate accumulator right without carry	RRC
RLC	none	Rotate accumulator left without carry	RLC
RAR	none	Rotate accumulator right with carry	RAR
RAL	none	Rotate accumulator left with carry	RAR
CMC	none	Compliments the carry flag	CMC

STC	none	Sets the carry flag	STC

In the table,
R stands for register
M stands for memory
Mc stands for memory contents

ROTATE Instructions

ROTATE is a logical operation of 8085 microprocessor. It is a 1 byte instruction. This instruction does not require any operand after the opcode. It operates the content of accumulator and the result is also stored in the accumulator. The Rotate instruction is used to rotating the bits of accumulator.

Types of ROTATE Instruction

There are 4 categories of the ROTATE instruction:
- Rotate accumulator left (RLC)
- Rotate accumulator left through carry (RAL)
- Rotate accumulator right (RRC)
- Rotate accumulator right through carry (RAR)

Among these four instructions; two are for rotating left and two are for rotating right. All of them are explain briefly in the following sections:

Rotate accumulator left (RLC)

In this instruction, each bit is shifted to the adjacent left position. Bit D7 becomes D0. Carry flag CY is modified according to the bit D7. For example:-

A = D7 D6 D5 D4 D3 D2 D2 D0

//before the instruction
A = 10101010; CY=0

//after 1st RLC
A = 01010101; CY=1

//after 2nd RLC
A = 10101010; CY=0

Rotate accumulator left through carry (RAL)

In this instruction, each bit is shifted to the adjacent left position. Bit D7 becomes the carry bit and the carry bit is shifted into D0. Carry flag CY is modified according to the bit D7. For example:
A = D7 D6 D5 D4 D3 D2 D2 D0

//before the instruction
A = 10101010; CY=0

//after 1st RAL
A = 01010100; CY=1

//after 2nd RAL
A = 10101001; CY=0

Rotate accumulator right (RRC)

In this instruction, each bit is shifted to the adjacent right position. Bit D0 becomes D7. Carry flag CY is modified according to the bit D0. For example:

A = D7 D6 D5 D4 D3 D2 D2 D0

//before the instruction
A = 10000001; CY=0

//after 1st RRC
A = 11000000; CY=1

//after 2nd RRC
A = 01100000; CY=0

Rotate accumulator right through carry (RAR)

In this instruction, each bit is shifted to the adjacent right position. Bit D0 becomes the carry bit and the carry bit is shifted into D7. Carry flag CY is modified according to the bit D0. For example:
A = D7 D6 D5 D4 D3 D2 D2 D0

//before the instruction
A = 10000001; CY=0

//after 1st RAR
A = 01000000; CY=1

//after 2nd RAR
A = 10100000; CY=0

Applications of ROTATE Instructions

The ROTATE instructions are primarily used in arithmetic multiply and divide operations and for serial data transfer. For example:
If A is 0000 1000 = 08H

By rotating 08H right: A = 0000 0100 = 04H
This is equivalent to *dividing by 2*.

By rotating 08H left: A = 0001 0000 = 10H
This is equivalent to *multiplying by 2*.

However, these procedures are invalid when logic 1 is rotated left from D7 to D0 or vice versa. For example, if 80H is rotated left it becomes 01H.

Data Transfer Instructions

Data transfer instructions are the instructions which transfers data in the microprocessor. They are also called copy instructions.

Following is the table showing the list of logical instructions:

Opcode	Operand	Explanation	Example
MOV	Rd, Rs	Rd = Rs	MOV A, B
MOV	Rd, M	Rd = Mc	MOV A, 2050
MOV	M, Rs	M = Rs	MOV 2050, A
MVI	Rd, 8-bit data	Rd = 8-bit data	MVI A, 50
MVI	M, 8-bit data	M = 8-bit data	MVI 2050, 50
LDA	16-bit address	A = contents at address	LDA 2050
STA	16-bit address	contents at address = A	STA 2050
LHLD	16-bit address	directly loads at H & L registers	LHLD 2050
SHLD	16-bit address	directly stores from H & L registers	SHLD 2050
LXI	r.p., 16-bit data	loads the specified register pair with data	LXI H, 3050
LDAX	r.p.	indirectly loads at the accumulator A	LDAX H
STAX	16-bit address	indirectly stores from the accumulator A	STAX 2050
XCHG	none	exchanges H with D, and L with	XCHG

		E	
PUSH	r.p.	pushes r.p. to the stack	PUSH H
POP	r.p.	pops the stack to r.p.	POP H
IN	8-bit port address	inputs contents of the specified port to A	IN 15
OUT	8-bit port address	outputs contents of A to the specified port	OUT 15

In the table,
R stands for register
M stands for memory
r.p. stands for register pair

Branching Instructions

Branching instructions refer to the act of switching execution to a different instruction sequence as a result of executing a branch instruction.

The three types of branching instructions are:
- Jump (unconditional and conditional)
- Call (unconditional and conditional)
- Return (unconditional and conditional)

Jump Instructions

The jump instruction transfers the program sequence to the memory address given in the operand based on the specified flag. Jump instructions are 2 types: Unconditional Jump Instructions and Conditional Jump Instructions.

Unconditional Jump Instructions

Transfers the program sequence to the described memory address.

Opcode	Operand	Explanation	Example
JMP	address	Jumps to the address	JMP 2050

Conditional Jump Instructions

Transfers the program sequence to the described memory address only if the condition in satisfied.

Opcode	Operand	Explanation	Example
JC	address	Jumps to the address if carry flag is 1	JC 2050
JNC	address	Jumps to the address if carry flag is 0	JNC 2050
JZ	address	Jumps to the address if zero flag is 1	JZ 2050
JNZ	address	Jumps to the address if zero flag is 0	JNZ 2050
JPE	address	Jumps to the address if parity flag is 1	JPE 2050
JPO	address	Jumps to the address if parity flag is 0	JPO 2050
JM	address	Jumps to the address if sign flag is 1	JM 2050
JP	address	Jumps to the address if sign flag 0	JP 2050

Call Instructions

The call instruction transfers the program sequence to the memory address given in the operand. Before transferring, the address of the next instruction after CALL is pushed onto the stack. Call instructions are 2 types: Unconditional Call Instructions and Conditional Call Instructions.

Unconditional Call Instructions

It transfers the program sequence to the memory address given in the operand.

Opcode	Operand	Explanation	Example
CALL	address	Unconditionally calls	CALL 2050

Conditional Call Instructions:

Only if the condition is satisfied, the instructions executes.

Opcode	Operand	Explanation	Example
CC	address	Call if carry flag is 1	CC 2050
CNC	address	Call if carry flag is 0	CNC 2050
CZ	address	Calls if zero flag is 1	CZ 2050
CNZ	address	Calls if zero flag is 0	CNZ 2050
CPE	address	Calls if carry flag is 1	CPE 2050
CPO	address	Calls if carry flag is 0	CPO 2050
CM	address	Calls if sign flag is 1	CM 2050
CP	address	Calls if sign flag is 0	CP 2050

Return Instructions

The return instruction transfers the program sequence from the subroutine to the calling program. Jump instructions are 2 types: Unconditional Jump Instructions and Conditional Jump Instructions.

Unconditional Return Instruction

The program sequence is transferred unconditionally from the subroutine to the calling program.

Opcode	Operand	Explanation	Example
RET	none	Return from the subroutine unconditionally	RET

Conditional Return Instruction

The program sequence is transferred unconditionally from the subroutine to the calling program only is the condition is satisfied.

Opcode	Operand	Explanation	Example
RC	none	Return from the subroutine if carry flag is 1	RC
RNC	none	Return from the subroutine if carry flag is 0	RNC
RZ	none	Return from the subroutine if zero flag is 1	RZ
RNZ	none	Return from the subroutine if zero flag is 0	RNZ
RPE	none	Return from the subroutine if parity flag is 1	RPE
RPO	none	Return from the subroutine if parity flag is 0	RPO
RM	none	Returns from the subroutine if sign flag is 1	RM
RP	none	Returns from the subroutine if sign flag is 0	RP

Difference between CALL and JUMP instructions

CALL instruction is used to call a subroutine. Subroutines are often used to perform tasks that need to be performed frequently. The JMP instruction is used to cause the PLC to skip over rungs.

The differences Between CALL and JUMP instructions are:

JUMP	CALL
Program control is transferred to a memory location which is in the main program	Program Control is transferred to a memory location which is not a part of main program
Immediate Addressing Mode	Immediate Addressing Mode + Register Indirect Addressing Mode
Initialization of SP (Stack Pointer) is not mandatory	Initialization of SP (Stack Pointer) is mandatory
Value of Program Counter (PC) is not transferred to stack	Value of Program Counter (PC) is transferred to stack
After JUMP, there is no return instruction	After CALL, there is a return instruction
Value of SP does not changes	Value of SP is decremented by 2
10 T states are required to execute this instruction	18 T states are required to execute this instruction
3 Machine cycles are required to execute this instruction	5 Machine cycles are required to execute this instruction

Reset Accumulator

There are 4 instructions to reset the accumulator in 8085. These instructions are:

Mnemonics	Comment
MVI A, 00	A <- 00
ANI 00	A AND 00
XRA A	A XOR A
SUB A	A <- A – A

MVI A, 00: instruction copies 00 to A.

ANI 00: instruction performs bit by bit AND operation of source operand (i.e. 00) to the destination operand (i.e. the accumulator A) and store the result in accumulator A.

XRA A: instruction performs XOR operation between source operand and destination operand and store the result in the accumulator. Here, source and destination operand both are same i.e. A. Therefore, the result after performing XOR operation, stored in the accumulator is 00.

SUB A: operation subtracts the contents of source operand (here, source register is A) from the contents of accumulator and store the result in the accumulator itself. Since, the source and destination operand are same. Therefore, accumulator A = 00.

Externally Initiated Operations

8085 microprocessor support some **externally initiated operations**, which are also known as **Peripheral operations**. Different external input/output devices or signals can initiate these type operations. In 8085 microprocessor chip, their individual pins are assigned.

Following are the some externally initiated operations:

RESET

This RESET key is used to clear the program counter and update with 0000H memory location. When this RESET pin is activated by any external key, then all the internal operations are suspended for that time. After that the execution of the program can begin at the zero memory address.

Interrupt

8085 microprocessor chip have some pins for interrupts like TRAP, RST 5.5, RST 6.5 and RST 7.5. The microprocessor can be interrupted from the normal instructions and asked to perform some other emergency operations, which are also known as Service routine. The microprocessor resumes its operation after the completion Service routine.

READY

The 8085 microprocessor has a pin called READY. If the signal at this READY pin is in low state then the microprocessor enters into the Wait state. The Input/Output devices that are connected to microprocessor are of different speed, which is need to be synchronized with the speed of microprocessor. This signal is used mainly to synchronize slower external devices with the microprocessor.

HOLD

When the HOLD pin is activated by an external signal, the microprocessor relinquishes control buses and allows the external peripheral to use them. For example, the HOLD signal is used Direct memory access (DMA) data transfer. In this DMA, the external Input/Output devices are directly communicate with the memory without interfering the processor every time.

Timing Diagram

MOV

Problem

Draw the timing diagram of the given instruction in 8085,
MOV B, C

Given instruction copies the contents of the source register into the destination register and the contents of the source register are not altered.

Example

MOV B, C
Opcode: MOV
Operand: B and C
B is the destination register and C is the source register whose contents need to be transferred to the destination register.

Algorithm

The instruction MOV B, C is of 1 byte; therefore the complete instruction will be stored in a single memory address. For example:
2000: MOV B, C
Only opcode fetching is required for this instruction and thus we need 4 T states for the timing diagram. For the opcode fetch the IO/M (low active) = 0, S1 = 1 and S0 = 1.

The timing diagram of MOV instruction is shown below:

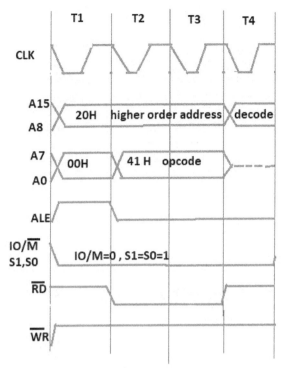

In Opcode fetch (t1-t4 T states)

00 – Lower bit of address where opcode is stored, i.e., 00
20 – Higher bit of address where opcode is stored, i.e., 20.
ALE – provides signal for multiplexed address and data bus. Only in t1 it used as address bus to fetch lower bit of address otherwise it will be used as data bus.
RD (low active) – signal is 1 in t1 & t4 as no data is read by microprocessor. Signal is 0 in t2 & t3 because here the data is read by microprocessor.
WR (low active) – signal is 1 throughout, no data is written by microprocessor.
IO/M (low active) – signal is 1 in throughout because the operation is performing on memory.
So and S1 – both are 1 in case of opcode fetching.

INR M

Problem

Draw the timing diagram of the given instruction in 8085,
INR M

The content present in the designated register/memory location (M) is incremented by 1 and the result is stored in the same place. If the operand is a memory location, it is specified by the contents of HL pair.

Example

INR M
Opcode: INR
Operand: M
M is the memory location (say 5000H) and suppose the data present at M (or 5000H) is 26H, which is need to be incremented by 1. Hex code- 34H

Algorithm

The instruction INR M is of 1 byte; therefore the complete instruction will be stored in a single memory address.

For example:
2000: INR M

The opcode fetch will be same as for other instructions in first 4 T states.

Only the Memory read and Memory Write need to be added in the successive T states.

For the opcode fetch the IO/M (low active) = 0, S1 = 1 and S0 = 1.
For the memory read the IO/M (low active) = 0, S1 = 1 and S0 = 0.
Also, only 3 T states will be required.
For the memory write the IO/M (low active) = 0, S1 = 0 and S0 = 1 and 3 T states will be required.

- 00: lower bit of address where opcode is stored, i.e., 00
- 20: higher bit of address where opcode is stored, i.e., 20.
- ALE: provides signal for multiplexed address and data bus. Only in t1 it used as address bus to fetch lower bit of address otherwise it will be used as data bus.
- RD (low active): signal is 1 in t1 & t4 as no data is read by microprocessor. Signal is 0 in t2 & t3 because here the data is read by microprocessor.
- WR (low active): Signal is 1 throughout, no data is written by microprocessor.
- IO/M (low active): Signal is 0 in throughout because the operation is performing on memory.
- So and S1: both are 1 in case of opcode fetching.

The timing diagram of INR M instruction is shown below:

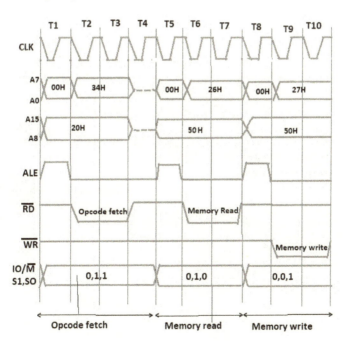

In Memory read (t5-t7 T states)

- **00:** lower bit of address where opcode is stored, i.e, 00
- **50:** higher bit of address where opcode is stored, i.e, 50.
- **ALE:** provides signal for multiplexed address and data bus. Only in t5 it used as address bus to fetch lower bit of address otherwise it will be used as data bus.
- **RD (low active):** signal is 1 in t5, no data is read by microprocessor. Signal is 0 in t6 & t7, data is read by microprocessor.
- **WR (low active):** signal is 1 throughout, no data is written by microprocessor.
- **IO/M (low active):** signal is 0 in throughout, operation is performing on memory.
- So and S1 – S1=1 and S0=0 for Read operation.

In Memory write (t8-t10 T states)

- **00:** lower bit of address where opcode is stored, i.e., 00
- **50:** higher bit of address where opcode is stored, i.e., 50.
- **ALE:** provides signal for multiplexed address and data bus. Only in t8 it used as address bus to fetch lower bit of address otherwise it will be used as data bus.
- **RD (low active):** signal is 1 throughout, no data is read by microprocessor.
- **WR (low active):** signal is 1 in t8, no data is written by microprocessor. Signal is 0 in t9 & t10, data is written by microprocessor.
- **IO/M (low active):** signal is 0 in throughout, operation is performing on memory.
- So and S1 – S1=0 and S0=1 for write operation.

Chapter 2 - 8085

Programming

8085 program to add two 8 bit numbers

Problem

Write an assembly language program to add two 8 bit numbers stored at address 2050 and address 2051 in 8085 microprocessor. The starting address of the program is taken as 2000.

Example

Input Data ⇨	F9	3B
Memory Address ⇨	2051	2050

Carry
⇩

Output Data ⇨	01	34
Memory Address ⇨	3051	3050

Algorithm
1. Load the first number from memory location 2050 to accumulator.
2. Move the content of accumulator to register H.
3. Load the second number from memory location 2051 to accumulator.
4. Then add the content of register B and accumulator using "ADD" instruction and storing result at 3050

5. The carry generated is recovered using "ADC" command and is stored at memory location 3051

Program

Address	Mnemonics	Comment
2000	LDA 2050	A<-[2050]
2003	MOV H, A	H<-A
2004	LDA 2051	A<-[2051]
2007	ADD H	A<-A+H
2006	MOV L, A	L←A
2007	MVI A 00	A←00
2009	ADC A	A←A+A+carry
200A	MOV H, A	H←A
200B	SHLD 3050	H→3051, L→3050
200E	HLT	

Explanation

1. LDA 2050 moves the contents of 2050 memory location to the accumulator.
2. MOV H, A copies contents of Accumulator to register H to A
3. LDA 2051 moves the contents of 2051 memory location to the accumulator.
4. ADD H adds contents of A (Accumulator) and H register (F9). The result is stored in A itself. For all arithmetic instructions A is by default an operand and A stores the result as well
5. MOV L, A copies contents of A (34) to L
6. MVI A 00 moves immediate data (i.e., 00) to A
7. ADC A adds contents of A (00), contents of register specified (i.e. A) and carry (1). As ADC is also an arithmetic operation, A is by default an operand and A stores the result as well
8. MOV H, A copies contents of A (01) to H

9. SHLD 3050 moves the contents of L register (34) in 3050 memory location and contents of H register (01) in 3051 memory location
10. HLT stops executing the program and halts any further execution

8085 program to add two 16 bit numbers

Write an assembly language program to add two 16 bit numbers by using:
- 8 bit operation
- 16 bit operation

Example

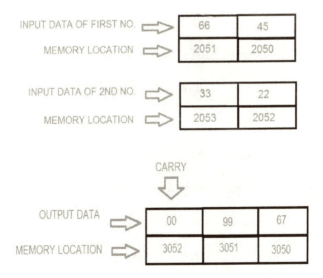

Addition of 16 bit numbers using 8 bit operation

It is a lengthy method and requires more memory as compared to 16 bit operation.

Algorithm
1. Load the lower part of first number in B register
2. Load the lower part of second number in A (accumulator)
3. Add both the numbers and store
4. Load the higher part of first number in B register
5. Load the higher part of second number in A (accumulator)
6. Add both the numbers with carry from the lower bytes (if any) and store at the next location

Program

Address	Mnemonics	Comment
2000	LDA 2050	A ← 2050
2003	MOV B, A	B ← A
2004	LDA 2052	A ← 2052
2007	ADD B	A ← A+B
2008	STA 3050	A → 3050
200B	LDA 2051	A ← 2051
200E	MOV B, A	B ← A
200F	LDA 2053	A ← 2053
2012	ADC B	A ← A+B+CY
2013	STA 3051	A → 3051

2016	HLT	Stops execution

Explanation

1. LDA 2050 stores the value at 2050 in A (accumulator)
2. MOV B, A stores the value of A into B register
3. LDA 2052 stores the value at 2052 in A
4. ADD B add the contents of B and A and store in A
5. STA 3050 stores the result in memory location 3050
6. LDA 2051 stores the value at 2051 in A
7. MOV B, A stores the value of A into B register
8. LDA 2053 stores the value at 2053 in A
9. ADC B add the contents of B, A and carry from the lower bit addition and store in A
10. STA 3051 stores the result in memory location 3051
11. HLT stops execution

Addition of 16 bit numbers using 16 bit operation

It is a very short method and less memory is also required as compared to 8 bit operation.

Algorithm
1. Load both the lower and the higher bits of first number at once
2. Copy the first number to another register pair
3. Load both the lower and the higher bits of second number at once
4. Add both the register pairs and store the result in a memory location

Program

Address	Mnemonics	Comment
2000	LHLD 2050	A ← 2050

2003	XCHG	D ← H & E ← L
2004	LHLD 2052	A ← 2052
2007	DAD D	H ← H+D & L ← L+E
2008	SHLD 3050	A → 3050
200B	HLT	Stops execution

Explanation

1. LHLD 2050 loads the value at 2050 in L register and that in 2051 in H register (first number)
2. XCHG copies the content of H to D register and L to S register
3. LHLD 2052 loads the value at 2052 in L register and that in 2053 in H register (second number)
4. DAD D adds the value of H with D and L with E and stores the result in H and L
5. SHLD 3050 stores the result at memory location 3050
6. HLT stops execution

8085 program to add three 16 bit numbers stored in registers

Problem

Write an assembly language program to add three 16 bit numbers stored in register HL, DE, BC and store the result in DE with minimum number of instructions.

Example

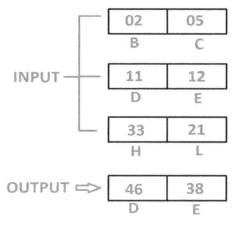

Assumptions

1. Numbers to be added are already stored in register HL, DE, BC
2. Numbers stored in register are such that final result should not be greater than FFFF

DAD D performs the following task:
H <- H + D
L <- L + E

DAD instruction take one argument and that argument can be register B, D, H or SP XCHG instruction exchanges the content of register D with H and E with L

Algorithm

1. Add the content of DE register in HL and store the result in HL by help of DAD instruction
2. Move the content of register B in D and C in E
3. Repeat step 1
4. Use XCHG instruction to swap the content of DE with HL. We will get the result in DE

Program

Address	Mnemonics	Comment
2000	DAD D	H <- H + D, L <- L + E
2001	MOV D, B	D <- B
2002	MOV E, C	E <- C
2003	DAD D	H <- H + D, L <- L + E
2004	XCHG	Swap HL with DE
2005	HLT	END

Explanation

1. DAD D adds the content of register D in H and register E in L and store the result in HL
2. MOV D, B moves the value of register B in register D
3. MOV E, C moves the value of register C in register E
4. Same as step 1
5. XCHG exchanges the content of register H with register D and L with E.
6. HLT stops executing the program and halts any further execution.

8085 program to add two BCD numbers

Problem

Write a program to add 2 BCD numbers where starting address is 2000 and the numbers is stored at 2500 and 2501 memory addresses and store sum into 2502 and carry into 2503 memory address.

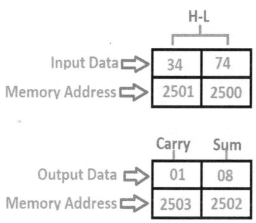

1. Load 00H in a register (for carry)
2. Load content from memory into register pair
3. Move content from L register to accumulator
4. Add content of H register with accumulator
5. Add 06H if sum is greater than 9 or Auxiliary Carry is not zero
6. If carry flag is not equal to 1, go to step 8
7. Increment carry register by 1
8. Store content of accumulator into memory
9. Move content from carry register to accumulator
10. Store content of accumulator into memory
11. Stop

Address	Mnemonics	Operands	Comment
2000	MVI	C, 00H	[C] <- 00H, carry

2002	LHLD	[2500]	[H-L] <- [2500]
2005	MOV	A, L	[A] <- [L]
2006	ADD	H	[A] <- [A] + [H]
2007	DAA		Add 06 if sum > 9 or AC = 1
2008	JNC	200C	Jump if no carry
200B	INR	C	[C] <- [C] + 1
200C	STA	[2502]	[A] -> [2502], sum
200F	MOV	A, C	[A] <- [C]
2010	STA	[2503]	[A] -> [2503], carry
2013	HLT		Stop

Explanation

Registers A, C, H and L are used for general purpose
1. MVI is used to move data immediately into any of registers (2 Byte)
2. LHLD is used to load register pair direct using 16-bit address (3 Byte instruction)
3. MOV is used to transfer the data from memory to accumulator (1 Byte)
4. ADD is used to add accumulator with any of register (1 Byte instruction)
5. STA is used to store data from accumulator into memory address (3 Byte instruction)
6. DAA is used to check if sum > 9 or AC = 1 add 06 (1 Byte instruction)
7. JNC is used jump if no carry to given memory location (3 Byte instruction)
8. INR is used to increase given register by 1 (1 Byte instruction)
9. HLT is used to halt the program

8085 program to subtract two 8-bit numbers with or without borrow

Write a program to subtract two 8-bit numbers with or without borrow where first number is at 2500 memory address and second number is at 2501 memory address and store the result into 2502 and borrow into 2503 memory address.

Example

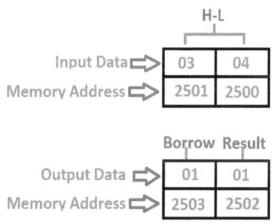

Algorithm

1. Load 00 in a register C (for borrow)
2. Load two 8-bit number from memory into registers
3. Move one number to accumulator
4. Subtract the second number with accumulator
5. If borrow is not equal to 1, go to step 7
6. Increment register for borrow by 1
7. Store accumulator content in memory
8. Move content of register into accumulator
9. Store content of accumulator in other memory location
10. Stop

Program

Address	Mnemonics	Operands	Comment
2000	MVI	C, 00	[C] <- 00
2002	LHLD	2500	[H-L] <- [2500]
2005	MOV	A, H	[A] <- [H]
2006	SUB	L	[A] <- [A] – [L]
2007	JNC	200B	Jump If no borrow
200A	INR	C	[C] <- [C] + 1
200B	STA	2502	[A] -> [2502], Result
200E	MOV	A, C	[A] <- [C]
2010	STA	2503	[A] -> [2503], Borrow
2013	HLT		Stop

Explanation

Registers A, H, L and C are used for general purpose:

1. MOV is used to transfer the data from memory to accumulator (1 Byte)
2. LHLD is used to load register pair directly using 16-bit address (3 Byte instruction)
3. MVI is used to move data immediately into any of registers (2 Byte)
4. STA is used to store the content of accumulator into memory(3 Byte instruction)
5. INR is used to increase register by 1 (1 Byte instruction)
6. JNC is used to jump if no borrow (3 Byte instruction)
7. SUB is used to subtract two numbers where one number is in accumulator(1 Byte)
8. HLT is used to halt the program.

8085 program to multiply two 8 bit numbers

Problem

Multiply two 8 bit numbers stored at address 2050 and 2051. Result is stored at address 3050 and 3051. Starting address of program is taken as 2000.

Example

Input Data ⇨	07	43
Memory Address ⇨	2051	2050

Output Data ⇨	01	D5
Memory Address ⇨	3051	3050

Algorithm

1. We are taking adding the number 43 seven (7) times in this example.
2. As the multiplication of two 8 bit numbers can be maximum of 16 bits so we need register pair to store the result.

Program

Address	Mnemonics	Comment
2000	LHLD 2050	H←2051, L←2050
2003	XCHG	H↔D, L↔E

2004	MOV C, D	C←D
2005	MVI D 00	D←00
2007	LXI H 0000	H←00, L←00
200A	DAD D	HL←HL+DE
200B	DCR C	C←C-1
200C	JNZ 200A	If Zero Flag=0, goto 200A
200F	SHLD 3050	H→3051, L→3050
2012	HLT	

Explanation

Registers used: A, H, L, C, D, E

1. LHLD 2050 loads content of 2051 in H and content of 2050 in L
2. XCHG exchanges contents of H with D and contents of L with E
3. MOV C, D copies content of D in C
4. MVI D 00 assigns 00 to D
5. LXI H 0000 assigns 00 to H and 00 to L
6. DAD D adds HL and DE and assigns the result to HL
7. DCR C decrements C by 1
8. JNZ 200A jumps program counter to 200A if zero flag = 0
9. SHLD stores value of H at memory location 3051 and L at 3050
10. HLT stops executing the program and halts any further execution

8085 program to divide two 16 bit numbers

Problem

Write an assembly language program in 8085 microprocessor to divide two 16 bit numbers.

Assumption

- Starting address of program: 2000
- Input memory location: 2050, 2051, 2052, 2053
- Output memory location: 2054, 2055, 2056, 2057.

Example

Input:

(2050H) = 04H
(2051H) = 00H
(2052H) = 02H
(2053H) = 00H

Output:

(2054H) = 02H
(2055H) = 00H
(2056H) = FEH
(2057H) = FFH

Result:

Hence we have divided two 16 bit numbers.

Algorithm

1. Initialize register BC as 0000H for Quotient.
2. Load the divisor in HL pair and save it in DE register pair.
3. Load the dividend in HL pair.
4. Subtract the content of accumulator with E register.
5. Move the content A to C and H to A.
6. Subtract with borrow the content of A with D.
7. Move the value of accumulator to H.
8. If CY=1, goto step 10, otherwise next step.
9. Increment register B and jump to step 4.

10. ADD both contents of DE and HL.
11. Store the remainder in memory.
12. Move the content of C to L & B to H.
13. Store the quotient in memory.

Program

Address	Mnemonics	Comment
2000	LXI B, 0000H	INITIALISE QUOTIENT AS 0000H
2003	LHLD 2052H	LOAD THE DIVISOR IN HL
2006	XCHG	EXCHANGE HL AND DE
2007	LHLD 2050	LOAD THE DIVIDEND
200B	MOV A, L	A<-L
200C	SUB E	A<-A-E
200D	MOV L, A	L<-A
200E	MOV A, H	A<-H
200F	SBB D	A<-A-D
2010	MOV H, A	H<-A
2011	JC 2018	JUMP WHEN CARRY
2014	INX B	B<-B+1
2015	JMP 200B	
2018	DAD D	HL<-DE+HL
2019	SHLD 2056	HL IS STORED IN MEMORY
201C	MOV L, C	L<-C
201D	MOV H, B	H<-B
201E	SHLD 2054	HL IS STORED IN MEMORY
2021	HLT	TERMINATES THE PROGRAM

Explanation

1. **LXI B, 0000H:** initialize BC register as 0000H.
2. **LHLD 2052H:** load the HL pair with address 2052.
3. **XCHG:** exchange the content of HL pair with DE pair register.
4. **LHLD 2050:** load the HL pair with address 2050.
5. **MOV A, L:** move the content of register L into register A.
6. **SUB E:** subtract the contents of register E with contents of accumulator.
7. **MOV L, A:** move the content of register A into register L.
8. **MOV A, H:** move the content of register H into register A.
9. **SBB D:** subtract the contents of register D with contents of accumulator with carry.
10. **MOV H, A:** move the content of register A into register H.
11. **JC 2018:** jump to address 2018 if there is carry.
12. **INX B:** increment BC register by one.
13. **JMP 200B:** jump to address 200B.
14. **DAD D:** add the contents of DE and HL pair.
15. **SHLD 2056:** stores the content of HL pair into memory address 2056 and 2057.
16. **MOV L, C:** move the content of register C into register L.
17. **MOV H, B:** move the content of register B into register H.
18. **SHLD 2054:** stores the content of HL pair into memory address 2054 and 2055.
19. **HLT:** terminates the execution of program.

8085 program to multiply two 8 bit numbers using logical instructions

Problem

Write an assembly language program multiply two 8 bit numbers and store the result at memory address 3050 in 8085 microprocessor.

Example

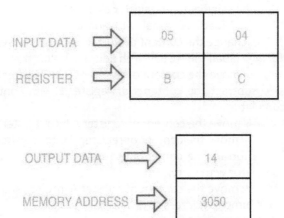

The value of accumulator (A) after using RLC instruction is:

$$A = 2^{n} * A$$

Where n = number of times RLC instruction is used.

Assumptions

Assume that the first number is stored at register B, and second number is stored at register C. And the result must not have any carry.

Algorithm

1. Assign the value 05 to register B
2. Assign the value 04 to register C
3. Move the content of B in A
4. Rotate accumulator left without carry
5. Rotate accumulator left without carry
6. Store the content of accumulator at memory address 3050
7. Halt of the program

Program

Address	Mnemonics	Comment
2000	MVI B 05	B <- 05
2002	MVI C 04	C <- 04
2004	MOV A, B	A <- B
2005	RLC	rotate the content of A without carry
2006	RLC	rotate the content of A without carry
2007	STA 3050	3050 <- A
200A	HLT	End of the program

Explanation

1. MVI B 05: assign the value 05 to B register.
2. MVI C 04: assign the value 04 to C register.
3. MOV A, B: move the content of register B to register A.
4. RLC: rotate the content of accumulator left without carry.
5. RLC: rotate the content of accumulator left without carry.
6. STA 3050: store the content of register A at memory location 3050
7. HLT: stops the execution of the program.

8085 program to find sum of digits of an 8 bit number

Problem

Write an assembly language program in 8085 microprocessor to find sum of digit of an 8 bit number.

Example

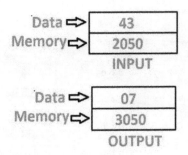

INPUT

OUTPUT

Assumptions

Addresses of input data and output data are 2050 and 3050 respectively.

Algorithm

1. Load value stored at memory location 2050 in accumulator A
2. Move the value of accumulator A in register B
3. Perform masking of nibbles i.e. do AND operation of accumulator A with OF by help of ANI instruction. We will get lower nibble value in accumulator A
4. Move the value of accumulator A in register C
5. Move the value of register B in accumulator A
6. Reverse the number which is stored in accumulator A by using RLC instruction 4 times and again do masking of nibbles as done in step 3
7. Add value of register C in accumulator A
8. Store the value of A in memory location 3050

Program

Address	Mnemonics	Comment
2000	LDA 2050	A <- M[2050]

2003	MOV B, A	B <- A
2004	ANI 0F	A <- A (AND) 0F
2006	MOV C, A	C <- A
2007	MOV A, B	A <- B
2008	RLC	Rotate left without carry
2009	RLC	Rotate left without carry
200A	RLC	Rotate left without carry
200B	RLC	Rotate left without carry
200C	ANI 0F	A <- A (AND) 0F
200E	ADD C	A <- A + C
200F	STA 3050	M[3050] <- A
2012	HLT	END

Explanation

Registers used: A, B, C
1. LDA 2050 loads the content of memory location 2050 in accumulator A
2. MOV B, A moves the value of accumulator A in register B
3. ANI 0F performs AND operation in value of accumulator A and 0F
4. MOV C, A moves the value of accumulator A in register C
5. MOV A, B moves the value of register B in accumulator A
6. RLC instruction rotates the value of accumulator A, left by 1 bit. Since it is performed 4 times therefore this will reverse the number i.e. swaps the lower order nibble with higher order nibble

7. Repeat step 3
8. ADD C adds the content of register of C in accumulator A
9. STA 3050 stores value of A in 3050
10. HLT stops executing the program and halts any further execution

8085 program to find the sum of a series

Problem

Write a program to find the sum of a series where series starts from 3001 memory address and count of series is at 3000 memory address where starting address of the given program is 2000 store result into 4000 memory address.

Example

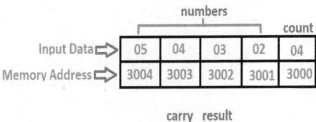

Algorithm

1. Move 00 to register B immediately for carry
2. Load the data of memory [3000] into H immediately
3. Move value of memory into register C
4. Decrease C by 1
5. Increase H-L pair by 1

6. Move value of memory into accumulator
7. Increase H-L pair by 1
8. Add value of memory with accumulator
9. Jump if no carry to step 11
10. Increase value of register B by one
11. Decrease register C by 1
12. Jump if not zero to step-7
13. Store content of accumulator into memory [4000] (result)
14. Move content of register B into accumulator
15. Store content of accumulator into memory [4001] (carry)
16. Stop

Program

Address	Mnemonics	Operands	Comment
2000	MVI	B, 00	[B] <- 00
2002	LXI	H, [3000]	[H-L] <- [3000]
2005	MOV	C, M	[C] <- [M]
2006	DCR	C	[C] <- [C] – 1
2007	INX	H	[H-L] <- [H-L] + 1
2008	MOV	A, M	[A] <- [M]
2009	INX	H	[H-L] <- [H-L] + 1
200A	ADD	M	[A] <- [A] + [M]
200B	JNC	200F	jump if no carry
200E	INR	B	[B] <- [B] + 1
200F	DCR	C	[C] <- [C] – 1
2010	JNZ	2009	jump if not zero
2013	STA	[4000]	result
2016	MOV	A, B	[A] <- [B]
2017	STA	[4001]	carry

201A	HLT		Stop

Explanation

Registers A, B, C and H are used for general purpose.
1. MVI is used to load an 8-bit given register immediately (2 Byte instruction)
2. LXI is used to load register pair immediately using 16-bit address (3 Byte instruction)
3. MOV is used to transfer the data from accumulator to register(any) or register(any) to accumulator (1 Byte)
4. RAR is used to shift 'A' right with carry (1 Byte instruction)
5. STA is used to store data from accumulator into memory direct using 16-bit address (3 Byte instruction)
6. INR is used to increase given register by 1 (1 Byte instruction)
7. JNC is used to jump to the given step if there is no carry (3 Byte instruction)
8. JNZ is used to jump to the given step if there is not zero (3 Byte instruction)
9. DCR is used to decrease given register by 1 (1 Byte instruction)
10. INX is used to increase register pair by 1 (1 Byte instruction)
11. ADD is used to add value of accumulator with the given value (1 Byte instruction)
12. HLT is used to halt the program

8085 program to find the sum of first n natural numbers

Problem

Write an assembly language program for calculating the sum of first n natural numbers using 8085 microprocessor.

Example

Input: 04H
Output: 0AH

as 01+02+03+04 = 10 in decimal => 0AH

Data	Result
201BH	201C
04H	0AH

The formula for calculating the sum of first n natural numbers is:

$$\frac{n(n + 1)}{2}$$

Algorithm

1. With n as the input, increment it to obtain n+1.
2. Multiply n with n+1.
3. Divide the product obtained by 2.

In 8085 microprocessor, no direct instruction exists to multiply two numbers, so multiplication is done by repeated addition as 4×5 is equivalent to 4+4+4+4+4 (i.e., 5 times).

Input: 04H
Add 04H 5 times
Product: 14H (20_{10})

Similarly, in 8085 microprocessor, no direct instruction exists to divide two numbers, so division is done by repeated subtraction.
Input: 14H

Keep on subtracting 2 from the input till it reduces to 0.
Since subtraction has to be performed 10_{10} times before 14H becomes 0, the quotient is 10_{10} => 0AH.

Steps

1. Load the data from the memory location (201BH, arbitrary choice) into the accumulator
2. Move this data into B
3. Increment the value in the accumulator by one and move it to the register C
4. Initialize the accumulator with 0
5. Multiplication: Keep adding B to accumulator. The number of times B has to be added is equal to the value of C
6. Initialize B with 00H. B will store the quotient of the division
7. Initialize C with 02H. This is the divisor for the division
8. Division: Keep subtracting C from A till A becomes 0. For each subtraction, increment B by one
9. The final answer is in B. Move it to A. Then store the value of A in 201CH (arbitrary choice again)
   201CH contains the final answer.

Address	Label	Mnemonics
2000H		LDA 201BH
2001H		
2002H		
2003H		MOV B, A
2004H		INR A
2005H		MOV C, A
2006H		MVI A, 00H
2007H		
2008H	LOOP1	ADD B
2009H		DCR C
200AH		JNZ LOOP1

200BH		
200CH		
200DH		MVI C, 02H
200EH		
200FH		MVI B, 00H
2010H		
2011H	LOOP2	INR B
2012H		SUB C
2013H		JNZ LOOP2
2014H		
2015H		
2016H		MOV A, B
2017H		STA 201CH
2018H		
2019H		
201AH		HLT

Store the value of n in 201BH. The sum can be found at 201CH.

8085 program to find the factorial of a number

Problem

Write an assembly language program for calculating the factorial of a number using 8085 microprocessor.

Example

Input : 04H
Output : 18H
as 04*03*02*01 = 24 in decimal => 18H

Data	Result
2000H	2001H
04H	18H

In 8085 microprocessor, no direct instruction exists to multiply two numbers, so multiplication is done by repeated addition as 4×3 is equivalent to 4+4+4 (i.e., 3 times).

Load 04H in D register -> Add 04H 3 times -> D register now contains 0CH -> Add 0CH 2 times -> D register now contains 18H -> Add 18H 1 time -> D register now contains 18H -> Output is 18H

	Registers B and D after each MULTIPLY function call			
B	04H	03H	02H	01H
D (Hexadecimal)	01H	04H	0CH	18H
D (Decimal)	01	04	12	24

Algorithm

1. Load the data into register B
2. To start multiplication set D to 01H
3. Jump to step 7
4. Decrements B to multiply previous number
5. Jump to step 3 till value of B>0
6. Take memory pointer to next location and store result
7. Load E with contents of B and clear accumulator
8. Repeatedly add contents of D to accumulator E times
9. Store accumulator content to D

10. Go to step 4

Program

Address	Label	Mnemonics	Comment
2000H	Data		Data Byte
2001H	Result		Result of factorial
2002H		LXI H, 2000H	Load data from memory
2005H		MOV B, M	Load data to B register
2006H		MVI D, 01H	Set D register with 1
2008H	FACTORIAL	CALL MULTIPLY	Subroutine call for multiplication
200BH		DCR B	Decrement B
200CH		JNZ FACTORIAL	Call factorial till B becomes 0
200FH		INX H	Increment memory
2010H		MOV M, D	Store result in memory
2011H		HLT	Halt
2100H	MULTIPLY	MOV E, B	Transfer contents of B to C
2101H		MVI A, 00H	Clear accumulator to store result
2103H	MULTIPLYLOOP	ADD D	Add contents of D to A
2104H		DCR E	Decrement E
2105H		JNZ MULTIPLYLOOP	Repeated addition
2108H		MOV D, A	Transfer contents of A to

			D
2109H		RET	Return from subroutine

Explanation

1. First set register B with data.
2. Set register D with data by calling MULTIPLY subroutine one time.
3. Decrement B and add D to itself B times by calling MULTIPLY subroutine as 4*3 is equivalent to 4+4+4 (i.e., 3 times).
4. Repeat the above step till B reaches 0 and then exit the program.
5. The result is obtained in D register which is stored in memory

8085 program to count number of once in the given 8-bit number

Problem

Write a program to count number of once in the given 8-bit number use register B to display the count of once where starting address is **2000** and the number is stored at **3000** memory address and store result into **3001** memory address.

Example

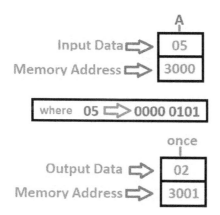

Algorithm

1. Move 00 to register B immediately for count
2. Move 08 to register C immediately for shifting
3. Load the data of memory [3000] into accumulator
4. Rotate 'A' right with carry
5. Jump if no carry to step-7
6. Otherwise increase register B by 1
7. Decrease register C by 1
8. Jump if not zero to step-4
9. Move content of register B into accumulator
10. Store content of accumulator into memory [3001] (number of count)
11. Stop

Program

Address	Mnemonics	Operands	Comment
2000	MVI	B, 00	[B] <- 00
2002	MVI	C, 08	[C] <- 08
2004	LDA	[3000]	[A] <- [3000]

2007	RAR		rotate 'A' right with carry
2008	JNC	200C	jump if no carry
200B	INR	B	[B] <- [B] + 1
200C	DCR	C	[C] <- [C] – 1
200D	JNZ	2007	jump if not zero
2010	MOV	A, B	[A] <- [B]
2011	STA	[3001]	number of once
2014	HLT		Stop

Explanation

Registers A, B and C are used for general purpose.

1. MVI is used to load an 8-bit given register immediately (2 Byte instruction)
2. LDA is used to load accumulator direct using 16-bit address (3 Byte instruction)
3. MOV is used to transfer the data from accumulator to register(any) or register(any) to accumulator (1 Byte)
4. RAR is used to shift 'A' right with carry (1 Byte instruction)
5. STA is used to store data from accumulator into memory direct using 16-bit address (3 Byte instruction)
6. INR is used to increase given register by 1 (1 Byte instruction)
7. JNC is used to jump to the given step if there is no carry (3 Byte instruction)
8. JNZ is used to jump to the given step if there is not zero (3 Byte instruction)
9. DCR is used to decrease given register by 1 (1 Byte instruction)
10. HLT is used to halt the program

8085 program to count the number of ones in contents of register B

Problem

Write an assembly language program to count the number of ones in contents of register B and store the result at memory location 3050.

Example

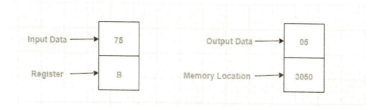

Algorithm

1. Convert the decimal number in Accumulator to its binary equivalent
2. Rotate the digits of the binary number right without carry
3. Apply a loop till count is not zero to change the values of D register and count
4. Copy the value of D register to accumulator and store the result

Program

Address	Mnemonics	Comment

2000	MVI B 75	B ← 75
2002	MVI C 08	C ← 75
2004	MVI D 00	D ← 00
2006	MOV A, B	A ← B
2007	RRC	Rotate right without carry
2008	JNC 200C	Jump if Not Carry
200B	INR D	D ← D+1
200C	DCR C	C ← C-1
200D	JNZ 2007	Jump if Not Zero
2010	MOV A, D	A ← D
2011	STA 3050	A → 3050
2014	HLT	Stops execution

Explanation

1. MVI B 75 moves 75 decimal number into B register
2. MVI C 08 moves 08 decimal number into C register, which is taken as counter as the number is of 8 bites
3. MVI D 00 moves 00 number into d register
4. MOV A, B moves the contents of B register into A (accumulator) register
5. RRC rotates the contents of A (which is 75 with binary equivalent 01110101) right

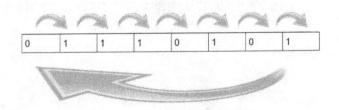

6. JNC 200C jumps to 200C address and perform the instructions written there if the carry flag is not zero
7. INR D increases the value of D register by adding one to its contents
8. DCR C decreases the value of C register by subtracting one from its contents
9. JNZ **2007** jumps to 2007 address and perform the instructions written there if the zero flag is not zero
10. MOV A, D moves the contents of B register into A register
11. STA 3050 store the contents of A at 3050 memory location
12. HLT stops execution

8085 program to count total even numbers in series of 10 numbers

Program

Write an assembly language program in 8085 microprocessor to count even numbers in series of 10 numbers.

Example

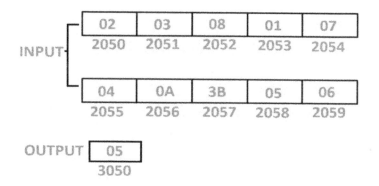

Assumption

Ten 8-bit numbers are stored from starting memory location 2050. Value of count is stored at memory location 3050.

Algorithm

1. Initialize register H with 20 and register L with 4F so that indirect memory points to memory location 204F.
2. Initialize register C with 00 and register D with 0A.
3. Increment indirect memory by 1.
4. Store value of M in accumulator A.
5. Check whether the content in A is even or odd by performing AND operation of A with 01.
6. If content of A is 00 after AND operation then number scanned was even, If so then increment C by 01 else if content of A is 01 after AND operation then number scanned was odd, If so then decrements D by 01.
7. Check if zero flag is not set i.e. ZF = 0 then jump to step 3 otherwise store value of C at memory location 3050.

Program

Address	Mnemonics	Comment
2000	LXI H 204F	H <- 20, L <- 4F
2003	MVI C, 00	C <- 00
2005	MVI D, 0A	D <- 0A
2007	INX H	M <- M + 01
2008	MOV A, M	A <- M
2009	ANI 01	A <- A (AND) 01
200B	JNZ 200F	Jump if ZF = 0

200E	INR C	C <- C + 01
200F	DCR D	D <- D – 01
2010	JNZ 2007	Jump if ZF = 0
2013	MOV A, C	A <- C
2014	STA 3050	M[3050] <- A
2017	HLT	END

Explanation

Registers A, B, C, D, H and L are used for general purpose.

1. LXI H 204F assigns 20 to H and 4F to L.
2. MVI C, 00 assigns 00 to C.
3. MVI D, 0A assigns 0A to D.
4. INX H increments indirect memory location M by 01.
5. MOV A, M moves content of M to A.
6. ANI 01 performs AND operation of A with 01 and store the result in A.
7. JNZ 200F jumps if ZF = 0 to memory location 200F.
8. INR C increments C by 01.
9. DCR D decrements D by 01.
10. JNZ 2007 jumps if ZF = 0 to memory location 2007.
11. MOV A, C moves the content of C to A.
12. STA 3050 stores the content of A to memory location 3050.
13. HLT stops executing the program and halts any further execution.

8085 program to find square root of a number

Problem

Write an assembly language program in 8085 microprocessor to find square root of a number.

Example

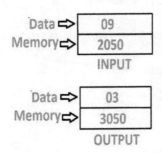

Assumptions

Number, whose square root we need to find is stored at memory location 2050 and store the final result in memory location 3050.

Algorithm

1. Assign 01 to register D and E
2. Load the value, stored at memory location 2050 in accumulator A
3. Subtract value stored at accumulator A from register D
4. Check if accumulator holds 0, if true then jump to step 8
5. Increment value of register D by 2
6. Increment value of register E by 1
7. Jump to step 3
8. Move value stored at register E in A
9. Store the value of A in memory location 3050

Program

Address	Mnemonics	Comment

2000	MVI D, 01	D <- 01
2002	MVI E, 01	E <- 01
2004	LDA 2050	A <- M[2050]
2007	SUB D	A <- A – D
2008	JZ 2011	Jump if ZF = 0 to memory location 2011
200B	INC D	D <- D + 1
200C	INC D	D <- D + 1
200D	INC E	E <- E + 1
200E	JMP 2007	Jump to memory location 2007
2011	MOV A, E	A <- E
2012	STA 3050	A -> M[3050]
2015	HLT	END

Explanation

Registers used: A, D, E

1. MVI D, 01 initializes register D with 01
2. MVI E, 01 initializes register E with 01
3. LDA 2050 loads the content of memory location 2050 in accumulator A
4. SUB D subtracts value of D from A
5. JZ 2011 makes jump to memory location 2011 if zero flag is set
6. INR D increments value of register D by 1. Since it is used two times, therefore value of D is incremented by 2
7. INR E increments value of register E by 1
8. JMP 2007 makes jump to memory location 2007

9. MOV A, E moves the value of register E in accumulator A
10. STA 3050 stores value of A in 3050
11. HLT stops executing the program and halts any further execution

8085 program to find 1's and 2's complement of 8-bit number

Problem

Write a program to find 1's and 2's complement of 8-bit number where starting address is 2000 and the number is stored at 3000 memory address and store result into 3001 and 3002 memory address.

Example

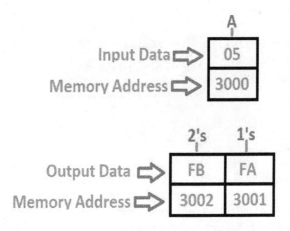

Algorithm

1. Load the data from memory 3000 into A (accumulator)
2. Complement content of accumulator
3. Store content of accumulator in memory 3001 (1's complement)
4. Add 01 to Accumulator content

5. Store content of accumulator in memory 3002 (2's complement)
6. Stop

Address	Mnemonics	Operands	Comment
2000	LDA	[3000]	[A] <- [3000]
2003	CMA		[A] <- [A^]
2004	STA	[3001]	1's complement
2007	ADI	01	[A] <- [A] + 01
2009	STA	[3002]	2's complement
200C	HLT		Stop

Explanation

1. A is an 8-bit accumulator which is used to load and store the data directly
2. LDA is used to load accumulator direct using 16-bit address (3 Byte instruction)
3. CMA is used to complement content of accumulator (1 Byte instruction)
4. STA is used to store accumulator direct using 16-bit address (3 Byte instruction)
5. ADI is used to add data into accumulator immediately (2 Byte instruction)
6. HLT is used to halt the program

8085 program to find 1's and 2's complement of 16-bit number

Problem

Write a program to find 1's and 2's complement of 16-bit number where starting address is 2000 and the number is stored at 3000 memory address and store result into 3002 and 3004 memory address.

Example

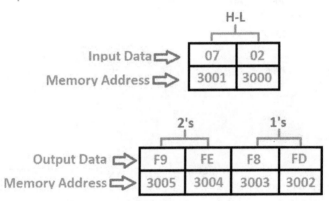

Algorithm

1. Load a 16-bit number from memory 3000 into a register pair (H-L)
2. Move content of register L to accumulator
3. Complement content of accumulator
4. Move content of accumulator to register L
5. Move content of register H to accumulator
6. Complement content of accumulator
7. Move content of accumulator to register H

8. Store content of register pair in memory 3002 (**1's** complement)
9. Increment content of register pair by 1
10. Store content of register pair in memory 3004 (**2's** complement)
11. Stop

Program

Address	Mnemonics	Operands	Comment
2000	LHLD	[3000]	[H-L] <- [3000]
2003	MOV	A, L	[A] <- [L]
2004	CMA		[A] <- [A^]
2005	MOV	L, A	[L] <- [A]
2006	MOV	A, H	[A] <- [H]
2007	CMA		[A] <- [A^]
2008	MOV	H, A	[H] <- [A]
2009	SHLD	[3002]	1's complement
200C	INX	H	[H-L] <- [H-L] + 1
200D	SHLD	[3004]	2's complement
2010	HLT		Stop

Explanation

1. A is an 8-bit accumulator which is used to load and store the data

2. LHLD is used to load register pair H-L direct using 16-bit address (3 Byte instruction)
3. MOV is used to transfer the data from accumulator to register(any) or register(any) to accumulator (1 Byte)
4. CMA is used to complement content of accumulator (1 Byte instruction)
5. SHLD is used to store data from register pair H-L into memory direct using 16-bit address (3 Byte instruction)
6. INX is used to increase H-L register pair by 1 (1 Byte instruction)
7. HLT is used to halt the program

8085 program to find 2's complement of the contents of Flag Register

Problem

Write an assembly language program in 8085 microprocessor to find 2's complement of the contents of Flag Register.

Algorithm

1. Initialize the value of Stack Pointer (SP) to 3999
2. Push the contents of PSW (Register pair formed by Accumulator and Flag Register) into the memory stack
3. Pop the contents from the stack into register pair BC
4. Move the contents of register C to A
5. Take 1's complement of the contents of A
6. Increment the contents of A by 1
7. Move the contents of A to C
8. Push the contents of register pair BC into the stack
9. Pop the contents of stack into PSW
10. Stop

Program

Address	Mnemonics	Comment

2000	LXI SP 3999	SP <- 3999
2003	PUSH PSW	PUSH value of Accumulator and Flag into the stack
2004	POP B	POP value from Top of stack into register pair BC
2005	MOV A, C	A <- C
2006	CMA	A = 1'S complement of A
2007	INR A	A = A + 1
2008	MOV C, A	C <- A
2009	PUSH B	PUSH value of register pair BC into stack
200A	POP PSW	POP value from Top of stack into Accumulator and Flag
200B	HLT	Stop

Explanation

1. LXI SP 3999 is used to initialize the value of Stack Pointer (SP) to 3999.
2. PUSH PSW is used to push the contents of PSW into the memory stack.
3. POP B is used to pop the contents from the top of stack into register pair BC.
4. MOV A, C moves the contents of register C to A.
5. CMA takes 1's complement of the contents of A.
6. INR A increments the contents of A by 1.
7. MOV C, A moves the contents of A to C.
8. PUSH B is used to push the contents of register pair BC into the stack.
9. POP PSW is used to pop the contents of stack into PSW.
10. HLT is used to end the program.

8085 programs to find 2's compliment with carry | Set 2

Problem

Find 2's compliment of an 8 bit number stored at address 2050. Result is stored at address 3050 and 3051. Starting address of program is taken as 2000.

Example

Input Data ⇨	07
Memory Address ⇨	2050

Output Data ⇨	00	F9
Memory Address ⇨	3051	3050

Algorithm

1. We are taking compliment of the number using CMA instruction.
2. Then adding 01 to the result.
3. The carry generated while adding 01 is stored at 3051.

Program

Address	Mnemonics	Comment

2000	LDA 2050	A←2050
2003	CMA	A←compliment of A
2004	INR A	A←A+01
2005	MOV L, A	L←A
2006	MVI A 00	A←00
2008	ADC A	A←A+A+Carry
2009	MOV H, A	H←A
200A	SHLD 3050	L→3050, H→3051
200D	HLT	

Explanation

Registers used: A, H, L
1. LDA 2050 loads content of 2050 in A
2. CMA compliments the contents of A
3. INR A increases A by 01
4. MOV L, A copies contents of A in L
5. MVI A 00 moves 00 in A
6. ADC A adds A, A, Carry and assigns it to A
7. MOV H, A copies contents of A in H
8. SHLD 3050 stores value of H at memory location 3051 and L at 3050
9. HLT stops executing the program and halts any further execution

Problem

Find 2's compliment of a 16 bit number stored at address 2050 and 2051. Result is stored at address 3050, 3051 and 3052. Starting address of program is taken as 2000.

Example

Input Data ⇨	07	3B
Memory Address ⇨	2051	2050

Output Data ⇨	00	F8	C5
Memory Address ⇨	3052	3051	3050

Algorithm

1. We are taking compliment of the numbers using CMA instruction.
2. Then adding 0001 to the result using INX instruction.
3. The carry generated while adding 0001 is stored at 3052.

Program

Address	Mnemonics	Comment
2000	LHLD 2050	L←2050, H←2051
2003	MOV A, L	A←L
2004	CMA	A←compliment of A
2005	MOV L, A	L←A
2006	MOV A, H	A←H
2007	CMA	A←Compliment of A
2008	MOV H, A	H←A
2009	INX H	HL←HL+0001

200A	MVI A 00	A←00
200C	ADC A	A←A+A+Carry
200D	SHLD 3050	L→3050, H→3051
2010	STA 3052	A→3052
2013	HLT	

Explanation

Registers used: A, H, L
1. LHLD 2050 loads content of 2051 in H and content of 2050 in L
2. MOV A, L copies contents of L in A
3. CMA compliments contents of A
4. MOV L, A copies contents of A in L
5. MOV A, H copies contents of H in A
6. CMA compliments contents of A
7. MOV H, A copies contents of A in H
8. INX H adds 0001 in HL
9. MVI A 00 moves 00 in A
10. ADC A adds A, A, Carry and stores result in A
11. SHLD 3050 stores value of H at memory location 3051 and L at 3050
12. STA 3052 stores value of A at memory location 3052
13. HLT stops executing the program and halts any further execution

8085 program to find nth power of a number

Problem

Write an assembly language code for calculating the nth power of a number using 8085 microprocessor.

Example
Input: Base=>02H
       Exponent=>03H

Output: 08H

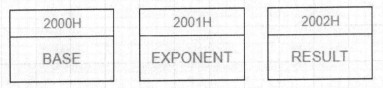

2000H	2001H	2002H
BASE	EXPONENT	RESULT

In 8085 microprocessor, no direct instruction exists to multiply two numbers, so multiplication is done by repeated addition as 4*4 is equivalent to 4+4+4+4(i.e. 4 times).

Load 02H(base) to register B and 03H(exponent) to register C -> set D register to 02H -> Add 02H B(i.e. 2) times -> D register now contains 04H -> Add 04H B(i.e. 2) times -> D register now contains 08H -> Output is 08H.

Registers B, C and D after each MULTIPLY function call

B	02H	02H	02H
C	03H	02H	01H
D	02H	02H+02H=04H	04H+04H=08H

Algorithm

1. Load the base into register B and exponent into register C.
2. To start multiplication set D to 01H.
3. Jump to step 7.
4. Decrements C.
5. Jump to step 3 till value of C>0.
6. Take memory pointer to next location and store result.
7. Load E with contents of B and clear accumulator.
8. Repeatedly add contents of D to accumulator E times.
9. Store accumulator content to D.
10. Go to step 4.

Program

Address	Label	Mnemonics	Comment
2000H	Base		Data Byte for base
2001H	Exponent		Data Byte for exponent
2002H	Result		Result of factorial
2003H		LXI H, 2000H	Load data from memory
2006H		MOV B, M	Load base to B register
2007H		INX H	Increment memory
2008H		MOV C, M	Load exponent to C register
2009H		MVI D, 01H	Set D register to 1
200BH	POWER_LOOP	CALL MULTIPLY	Subroutine call for multiplication
200EH		DCR C	Decrement C
200FH		JNZ POWER_LOOP	Call power_loop till C becomes 0
2012H		INX H	Increment memory
2013H		MOV M, D	Store result in memory
2014H		HLT	Halt
2100H	MULTIPLY	MOV E, B	Transfer contents of B to E
2101H		MVI A, 00H	Clear accumulator to store result
2103H	MULTIPLYLOOP	ADD D	Add contents of D to A

2104H		DCR E	Decrement E
2105H		JNZ MULTIPLYLOOP	Repeated addition
2108H		MOV D, A	Transfer contents of A to D
2109H		RET	Return from subroutine

Explanation

1. Set register B with base and register C with exponent.
2. Set register D with base by calling MULTIPLY subroutine one time.
3. Decrement C and add D to itself B times by calling MULTIPLY subroutine.
4. Repeat the above step till C reaches 0 and then exit the program.
5. The result is obtained in D register which is stored in memory

8085 program to check whether the given number is even or odd

Problem

Write an assembly language program in 8085 microprocessor to check whether the 8 bit number which is stored at memory location 2050 is even or odd. If even, store 22 at memory location 3050 otherwise store 11 at memory location 3050.

Example

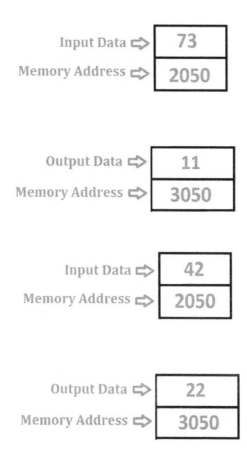

Input Data ⇨ 73
Memory Address ⇨ 2050

Output Data ⇨ 11
Memory Address ⇨ 3050

Input Data ⇨ 42
Memory Address ⇨ 2050

Output Data ⇨ 22
Memory Address ⇨ 3050

A number is said to be odd if its lower bit is 1 otherwise even. Therefore to identify whether the number is even or odd, we perform AND operation with 01 by the help of ANI instruction. If number is odd then we will get 01 otherwise 00 in accumulator. ANI instruction also affect the flags of 8085. Therefore if accumulator contains 00 then zero flag becomes set otherwise reset.

Algorithm
1. Load the content of memory location 2050 in accumulator A.
2. Perform AND operation with 01 in value of accumulator A by the help of ANI instruction.

3. Check if zero flag is set, i.e if ZF = 1 then store 22 in accumulator A otherwise store 11 in A.
4. Store the value of A in memory location 3050

Program

Address	Mnemonics	Comment
2000	LDA 2050	A <- M[2050]
2003	ANI 01	A <- A (AND) 01
2005	JZ 200D	Jump if ZF = 1
2008	MVI A 11	A <- 11
200A	JMP 200F	Jump to memory location
200D	MVI A 22	A <- 22
200F	STA 3050	M[3050] <- A
2012	HLT	END

Explanation

Registers used: A
1. LDA 2050 loads the content of memory location 2050 in accumulator A
2. ANI 01 performs AND operation between accumulator A and 01 and store the result in A
3. JZ 200D jumps to memory location 200D if ZF = 1
4. MVI A 11 assigns 11 to accumulator
5. JMP 200F jumps to memory location 200F
6. MVI A 22 assigns 22 to accumulator
7. STA 3050 stores value of A in 3050

8. **HLT** stops executing the program and halts any further execution

8085 program to find square of a 8 bit number

Problem

Write an assembly language program in 8085 microprocessor to find square of 8 bit number.

Example

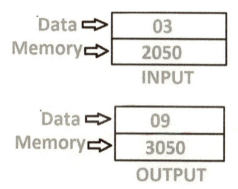

Assumption

Addresses of input data and out data are 2050 and 3050 respectively.

Approach

Combine the content of registers H and L, the resultant content can be used to indirectly point to memory location and that memory location is specified by M. To find square of any number, keep on adding that number in accumulator A which initially contains 0 by that number of times whose square we need to find.

Algorithm

1. Assign 20 to register H, 50 to register L and 00 to accumulator A
2. Load the content of memory location which is specified by M in register B
3. Add content of M in accumulator A and decrement value of B by 01
4. Check if B holds 00, if true then store the value of A at memory location 3050 otherwise go to step 3

Program

Address	Mnemonics	Comment
2000	MVI H 20	H <- 20
2002	MVI L 50	L <- 50
2004	MVI A 00	A <- 00
2006	MOV B, M	B <- M
2007	ADD M	A <- A + M
2008	DCR B	B <- B – 01
2009	JNZ 2007	Jump if ZF = 0
200C	STA 3050	M[3050] <- A
200F	HLT	END

Explanation

Registers used A, H, L, B and indirect memory M:
1. MVI H 20 initializes register H with 20
2. MVI L 50 initializes register L with 50
3. MVI A 00 initializes accumulator A with 00
4. MOV B, M moves the content of memory location which is indirectly specified by M in register B
5. ADD M adds the content of memory location which is indirectly specified by M in accumulator A
6. DCR B decrements value of register B by 1
7. JNZ 2007 jumps to memory location 2007 if ZF = 0, i.e. register B does not contain 0
8. STA 3050 stores value of A in 3050
9. HLT stops executing the program and halts any further execution

8085 program to find minimum value of digit in the 8 bit number

Problem

Write an assembly language program in 8085 microprocessor to find minimum value of digit in the 8 bit number.

Example

Assume 8 bit number is stored at memory location 2050, and minimum value digit is stored at memory location 3050.

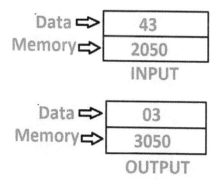

Algorithm

1. Load the content of memory location 2050 in accumulator A.
2. Move the content of A in register B.
3. Perform AND operation of content of A with oF and store the result in A.
4. Move the content of A in register C.
5. Move the content of B in A.
6. Reverse the content of A by using RLC instruction 4 times.
7. Perform AND operation of content of A with oF and store the result in A.
8. Compare the contents of A and C by help of CMP C instruction.
9. Check if carry flag is set then jump to memory location 2013 otherwise move the content of C in A. Go to memory location 2013.
10. Store the value of A in memory location 3050.

Note: CMP C instruction compares the value of A and C. If A>C then carry flag becomes reset otherwise set.

Program

Address	Mnemonics	Comment
2000	LDA 2050	A <- M[2050]
2003	MOV B, A	B <- A
2004	ANI oF	A <- A (AND) oF
2006	MOV C, A	C <- A
2007	MOV A, B	A <- B
2008	RLC	Rotate content of accumulator right by 1 bit without carry
2009	RLC	Rotate content of accumulator right by 1 bit without carry

200A	RLC	Rotate content of accumulator right by 1 bit without carry
200B	RLC	Rotate content of accumulator right by 1 bit without carry
200C	ANI 0F	A <- A (AND) 0F
200E	CMP C	A – C
200F	JC 2013	Jump if CY = 1
2012	MOV A, C	A <- C
2013	STA 3050	M[3050] <- A
2016	HLT	END

Explanation

Registers A, B, C are used for general purpose.

1. LDA 2050: loads the contents of memory location 2050 in A.
2. MOV B, A: moves the content of A in B.
3. ANI 0F: perform AND operation between contents of A and value 0F.
4. MOV C, A: moves the content of A in C.
5. MOV A, B: moves the content of B in A.
6. RLC: shift the content of A left by 1 bit without carry. Use this instruction 4 times to reverse the content of A.
7. ANI 0F: perform AND operation between contents of A and value 0F.
8. CMP C: compare contents of A, C and update the value of carry flag accordingly.
9. JC 2013: jump to memory location 2013 if CY = 1.
10. MOV A, C: moves the content of C in A.
11. STA 3050: stores the content of A in memory location 3050.
12. HLT: stops executing the program and halts any further execution.

8085 program to find maximum and minimum of 10 numbers

Problem

Write an assembly language program in 8085 microprocessor to find maximum and minimum of 10 numbers.

Example

List :	42H	21H	01H	1FH	FFH	25H	32H	34H	0AH	ABH

Minimum: 01H, Maximum: FFH
In CMP instruction
If Accumulator > Register then carry and zero flags are reset
If Accumulator = Register then zero flag is set
If Accumulator < Register then carry flag is set

Assumption

List of numbers from 2050H to 2059H and output at 2060H and 2061H.

Algorithm

1. Maximum number is stored in B register and minimum in C register
2. Load counter in D register
3. Load starting element in Accumulator, B and C register
4. Compare Accumulator and B register
5. If carry flag is not set then transfer contents of Accumulator to B. Else, compare Accumulator with C register, if carry flag is set transfer contents of Accumulator to C
6. Decrement D register
7. If D>0 take next element in Accumulator and go to point 4
8. If D=0, store B and C register in memory
9. End of program

Program

Address	Label	Mnemonics	Comment
2000H		LXI H, 2050H	Load starting address of list
2003H		MOV B, M	Store maximum
2004H		MOV C, M	Store minimum
2005H		MVI D, 0AH	Counter for 10 elements
2007H	LOOP	MOV A, M	Retrieve list element in Accumulator
2008H		CMP B	Compare element with maximum number
2009H		JC MIN	Jump to MIN if not maximum
200CH		MOV B, A	Transfer contents of A to B as A > B
200DH	MIN	CMP C	Compare element with minimum number
200EH		JNC SKIP	Jump to SKIP if not minimum
2011H		MOV C, A	Transfer contents of A to C if A < minimum
2012H	SKIP	INX H	Increment memory
2013H		DCR D	Decrement counter
2014H		JNZ LOOP	Jump to LOOP if D > 0
2017H		LXI H, 2060H	Load address to store maximum
201AH		MOV M, B	Move maximum to 2060H
201BH		INX H	Increment memory

201CH		MOV M, C	Move minimum to 2061H
201DH		HLT	Halt

1. One by one all elements are compared with B and C register.
2. Element is compared with maximum, if it greater than maximum then it is stored in B register. Else, it is compared with minimum and if it is less than minimum then it stored in C register.
3. Loop executes 10 number of times.
4. At the end of 10 iterations, maximum and minimum are stored at 2060H and 2061H respectively.

8085 program to find larger of two 8 bit numbers

Problem

Write a program in 8085 microprocessor to find out larger of two 8-bit numbers, where numbers are stored in memory address 2050 and 2051, and store the result into memory address 3050.

Example

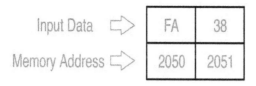

Input Data ⇨ | FA | 38
Memory Address ⇨ | 2050 | 2051

Output Data ⇨ | FA
Memory Address ⇨ | 3050

Algorithm

1. Load two numbers from memory 2050 & 2051 to register L and H.
2. Move one number (H) to Accumulator A and subtract other number (L) from it.
3. If result is positive then move the number (H) to A and store value of A at memory address 3050 and stop else move the number (L) to A and store value of A at memory address 3050 and stop.

Program

Address	Mnemonics	Comment
2000	LHLD 2050	H<-(data at 2051)&L<-(data at 2050)
2003	MOV A, H	A<-H
2004	SUB L	A<-A-L
2005	JP 200D	JUMP TO 200D IF NO. IS POSITIVE

2008	MOV A, L	A<-L
2009	STA 3050	A->(in memory 3050)
200C	HLT	STOP
200D	MOV A, H	A<-H
200E	STA 3050	A->(in memory 3050)
2011	HLT	STOP

Explanation

1. LHLD 2050: load data from memory 2050 & 2051 to register L and H.
2. MOV A, H: transfer contents of register H to A.
3. SUB L: subtract contents of register L from A and store it to A.
4. JP 200D: jump to address 200D if result is positive.
5. MOV A, L: transfer contents of register L to A.
6. STA 3050: store data of A to memory address 3050.
7. HLT: END.
8. MOV A, H: transfer contents of register H to A.
9. STA 3050: store data of A to memory address 3050.
10. HLT: END.

8085 program to find smallest number between two numbers

Problem

Write an assembly language program to find smallest number between two numbers.

Example

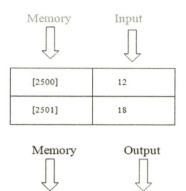

Memory	Input
[2500]	12
[2501]	18

Memory	Output
[2502]	12

Algorithm

1. Load the content from memory location
2. Move content of Accumulator into Register B
3. Load the content from Memory location
4. Compare the content of Register B
5. If carry flag is equal to 1 go to step 7
6. Move content of Register B into Accumulator
7. Store the content into Memory
8. End of program

Program

Address	Mnemonics	Operand	Comment
2000	LDA	[2500]	[A]<-[2500]
2003	MOV B, A		[B]<-[A]
2004	LDA	2501	[A]<-[2501]

2007	CMP B		[A]<-[A]-[B]
2008	JC *	[200C]	jump carry
200B	MOV B, A		[A]<-[B]
200C	STA	[2502]	[A]->[2502]
200F	HLT		STOP

Explanation

1. LDA is used to load accumulator (3 Byte instruction).
2. CMP is used to compare the content of accumulator (1 Byte instruction).
3. STA is used to store accumulator direct using 16-bit address (3 Byte instruction).
4. JC jump if carry (3 Byte instruction).

8085 program to find maximum of two 8 bit numbers

Problem

Write an assembly language program to find maximum of two 8 bit numbers in 8085 microprocessor.

Assumptions

Starting memory locations and output memory locations are 2050, 2051 and 3050 respectively.

Example

Input data	15	25
Memory address	2050	2051

Output data	25
Memory address	3050

Algorithm

Load value in the accumulator
1. Then, copy the value to any of the register
2. Load next value in the accumulator
3. Compare both values
4. Check carry flag, if reset then jump to the required address to store the value
5. Copy the result in the accumulator
6. Store the result at the required address

Program

Address	Mnemonics	Comment	
2000	LDA 2050	A<-25	
2003	MOV B, A	B<-25	
2004	LDA 2051	A<-15	
2007	CMP B	A-B	

2008	JNC 200C	Jump if Carry flag is Reset(Carry flag = 0)
200B	MOV A, B	A<-25
200C	STA 3050	3050<-25
200F	HLT	Terminates the program

Explanation

1. LDA 2050: loads value at memory location 2050
2. MOV B, A: assigns value of A to B
3. LDA 2051: loads value at memory location 2051
4. CMP B: compare values by subtracting B from A
5. JNC 200C: jump at memory location 200C if carry flag is Reset(Carry flag = 0)
6. STA 3050: store result at memory location 3050
7. HLT: terminates the program

8085 program to reverse 8 bit number

Problem

Write an assembly language program in 8085 microprocessor to reverse 8 bit number.

Example

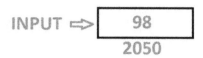

INPUT ⇨ | 98
2050

OUTPUT ⇨ | 89
3050

Assume that number to be reversed is stored at memory location 2050, and reversed number is stored at memory location 3050.

Algorithm

1. Load content of memory location 2050 in accumulator A
2. Use RLC instruction to shift content of A by 1 bit without carry. Use this instruction 4 times to reverse the content of A
3. Store content of A in memory location 3050

Program

Address	Mnemonics	Comment
2000	LDA 2050	A <- M[2050]
2003	RLC	Shift content of accumulator left by 1 bit without carry
2004	RLC	Shift content of accumulator left by 1 bit without carry
2005	RLC	Shift content of accumulator left by 1 bit without carry
2006	RLC	Shift content of accumulator left by 1 bit without carry
2007	STA 3050	M[2050] <- A

200A	HLT	END

Register used: A
1. LDA 2050: load value of memory location 2050 in Accumulator A.
2. RLC: shift content of accumulator left by 1 bit without carry.
3. RLC: shift content of accumulator left by 1 bit without carry.
4. RLC: shift content of accumulator left by 1 bit without carry.
5. RLC: shift content of accumulator left by 1 bit without carry.
6. STA 3050: store content of A in memory location 3050.
7. HLT: stops executing the program and halts any further execution.

8085 program to reverse 16 bit number

Problem

Write an assembly language program in 8085 microprocessor to reverse 16 bit number.

Example

Assume 16 bit number is stored at memory location 2050 and 2051.

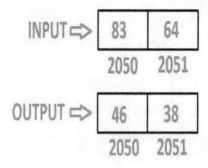

Algorithm

1. Load contents of memory location 2050 in register L and contents of memory location 2051 in register H
2. Move contents of L in accumulator A
3. Reverse the contents of A by executing RLC instruction 4 times
4. Move the contents of A in L
5. Move the contents of H in A
6. Reverse the contents of A by executing RLC instruction 4 times
7. Move the contents of L in H
8. Move the contents of A in L
9. Store the content of L in memory location 2050 and contents of H in memory location 2051

Program

Address	Mnemonics	Comment
2000	LHLD 2050	L <- M[2050], H <- M[2051]
2003	MOV A, L	A <- L
2004	RLC	Rotate accumulator content left by 1 bit without carry
2005	RLC	Rotate accumulator content left by 1 bit without carry
2006	RLC	Rotate accumulator content left by 1 bit without carry
2007	RLC	Rotate accumulator content left by 1 bit without carry
2008	MOV L, A	L <- A

2009	MOV A, H	A <- H
200A	RLC	Rotate accumulator content left by 1 bit without carry
200B	RLC	Rotate accumulator content left by 1 bit without carry
200C	RLC	Rotate accumulator content left by 1 bit without carry
200D	RLC	Rotate accumulator content left by 1 bit without carry
200E	MOV H, L	H <- L
200F	MOV L, A	L <- A
2010	SHLD 2050	M[2050] <- L, M[2051] <- H
2013	HLT	END

Explanation

Registers A, H, L are used for general purpose.

1. LHLD 2050: loads contents of memory location 2050 in L and 2051 in H.
2. MOV A, L: moves content of L in A.
3. RLC: shift the content of A left by one bit without carry. Repeat the current instruction 4 times so that contents of A get reversed.
4. MOV L, A: moves the content of A in L.
5. MOV A, H: moves the content of H in A.
6. RLC: shift the content of A left by one bit without carry. Repeat the current instruction 4 times so that contents of A get reversed.
7. MOV H, L: moves the content of L in H.

8. MOV L, A: moves the content of A in L.
9. SHLD 2050: stores the content of L in 2050 and H in 2051.
10. HLT: stops executing the program and halts any further execution.

8085 program to add numbers in an array

Problem

Write an assembly language program to add hexadecimal numbers stored in continuous memory or in an array.

Assumption

Suppose the size of the array is stored at memory location 2050 and the base address of the array is 2051. The sum will be stored at memory location 3050 and carry will be stored at location 3051.

Example

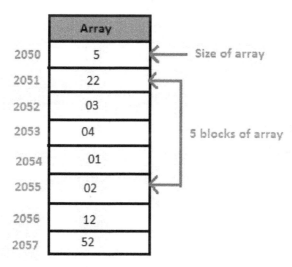

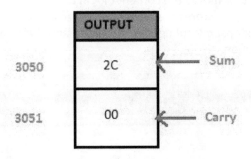

	OUTPUT	
3050	2C	Sum
3051	00	Carry

Algorithm

1. Load the base address of the array in HL register pair.
2. Use the size of the array as a counter.
3. Initialize accumulator to 00.
4. Add content of accumulator with the content stored at memory location given in HL pair.
5. Decrease counter on each addition.

Program

Address	Mnemonics	Comment
2000	LDA 2050	A <- [2050]
2003	MOV B, A	B <- A
2004	LXI H, 2051	H <- 20 and L <- 51
2007	MVI A, 00	A <- 00
2009	MVI C, 00	C <- 00
200B	ADD M	A <- A+M

200C	INR L	M <- M+1
200D	JNC 2011	
2010	INR C	C <- C+1
2011	DCR B	B <- B-1
2012	JNZ 200B	
2015	STA 3050	3050 <- A
2018	MOV A, C	A <- C
2019	STA 3051	3051 <- A
201C	HLT	Terminates the program

Explanation

1. LDA 2050: load accumulator with content of location 2050
2. MOV B, A: copy contents of accumulator to register B
3. LXI H, 2051: store 20 to H register and 51 to L register
4. MVI A, 00: store 00 to accumulator
5. MVI C, 00: store 00 to register C
6. ADD M: add accumulator with the contents of memory location given in HL register pair
7. INR L: increase address by 1
8. JNC 2011: if not carry, jump to location 2011 otherwise to the location given in PC
9. INR C: increase content of register C by 1
10. DCR B: decrease content of register B by 1
11. JNZ 200B: if not zero, jump to location 200B otherwise to the location given in PC
12. STA 3050: store contents of accumulator to memory location 3050
13. MOV A, C: copy contents of register C to accumulator
14. STA 3051: store contents of accumulator to memory location 3051
15. HLT: terminates the program

8085 program to find the sum of series of even numbers

Problem

Calculate the sum of series of even numbers from the given list of numbers. The length of the list is in memory location 2200H and the series begins from memory location 2201H. Result will store at memory location 2210H.

2200H= 4H
2201H= 20H
2202H= l5H
2203H= l3H
2204H= 22H
Output
Result 2210H = 42H

Program

Mnemonics	Operands	Comment
LDA	2200H	[A] <- 2200H
MOV	C, A	Initialize counter
MVI	B, 00H	sum = 0
LXI	H, 2201H	Initialize pointer
BACK:	MOV A, M	Get the number
ANI	01H	Mask Bit I to Bit7

JNZ	SKIP	Don't add if number is ODD
MOV	A, B	Get the sum
ADD	M	SUM = SUM + data
MOV	B, A	Store result in B register
SKIP:	INX H	increment pointer
DCR	C	Decrement counter
JNZ	BACK	if counter o repeat
STA	2210H	store sum
HLT		Terminate program execution

Explanation

A microprocessor is a computer processor that incorporates the functions of a central processing unit on a single integrated circuit.
1. A is an 8-bit accumulator which is used to load and store the data directly.
2. LDA is used to load accumulator direct using 16-bit address (3 Byte instruction).
3. Instructions like MOV, MVI, LDA are the data transfer instructions.
4. ADD is used to add data.
5. HLT is used to halt the program.

8085 program to convert an 8 bit number into Grey number

Problem

Write an assembly language program in 8085 which convert an 8 bit number into grey number

Example

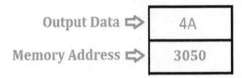

Assumption

8 bit number (input) is stored at memory location 2050 and output to be stored at memory location 3050.

Algorithm

1. Load the content of memory location 2050 in Accumulator
2. Reset carry flag i.e. CY = 0
3. Rotate the contents of Accumulator right by 1 bit with carry and perform xor operation with initial value of input
4. Store the result at memory location 3050

Program

Address	Mnemonics	Comment

2000	LDA 2050	A <- M[2050]
2003	MOV B, A	B <- A
2004	STC	CY = 1
2005	CMC	CY <- complement of CY
2006	RAR	Rotate 1 bit right with carry
2007	XRA B	A <- A XOR B
2008	STA 3050	M[3050] <- A
200B	HLT	End of program

Explanation

1. LDA 2050 loads the content of memory location 2050 in accumulator
2. MOV B, A transfers the content of register A in register B
3. STC sets the carry flag i.e. CY becomes 1
4. CMC complements the carry flag i.e. CY becomes 0
5. RAR rotate the content of accumulator by 1 bit along with carry flag
6. XRA B performs the XOR operation in values of register A and register B and store the result in A
7. STA 3050 stores the value of accumulator in memory location 3050
8. HLT stops executing the program and halts any further execution

8085 program to convert binary numbers to gray

Problem

Write an assembly language program in 8085 microprocessor to convert binary numbers to gray.

Example

| Input Data | ⇨ | 04 |
| Memory Address | ⇨ | 2050 |

| Output Data | ⇨ | 06 |
| Memory Address | ⇨ | 3050 |

Algorithm

1. Set the Carry Flag (CY) to 0.
2. Load the data from address 2050 in A.
3. Move the data of A (accumulator) into register B.
4. Rotate the bits of A to right.
5. XOR the contents of register A and B.
6. Store the result at memory address 3050.
7. Stop.

Program

Address	Mnemonics	Comment

2000	STC	CY <- 1
2001	CMC	CY <- 1's Compliment of CY
2002	LDA 2050	A <- 2050
2005	MOV B,A	B <- A
2006	RAR	Rotate accumulator right with carry
2007	XRA B	A = A XOR B
2008	STA 3050	3050 <- A
200B	HLT	Stop

Explanation

1. STC is used to set carry flag (CY) to 1.
2. CMC is used to take 1's compliment of the contents of carry flag (CY).
3. LDA 2050 is used load the data from address 2050 in A.
4. MOV B, A is used to move the data of A into B.
5. RAR is used to rotate the bits of A along with carry flag (CY) to right one time.
6. XRA B is used to perform XOR operation between the contents of register A and B.
7. STA 3050 is used to store the contents of A to 3050.
8. HLT is used end the program.

8085 program to convert gray to binary

Problem

Write an assembly language program in 8085 microprocessor to convert gray numbers to binary.

Example

Input Data	⇨	0B
Memory Address	⇨	2050

Output Data	⇨	0D
Memory Address	⇨	3050

Algorithm

1. Load the data from address 2050 in A
2. Move the data 07 in C
3. Move the data of A to B
4. Extract the MSB (Most Significant Bit) of data available in A
5. Rotate the bits of A to right
6. Take AND between data in A and 7F
7. Take XOR between the data present in A and B
8. Decrements the contents of C
9. If Zero Flag (ZF) is not set go to step 4 else go to step 9
10. Store the result at memory address 3050
11. Stop

Program

Address	Mnemonics	Comment
2000	LDA 2050	A <- 2050
2003	MVI C, 07	C <- 07

2005	MOV B, A	B <- A
2006	ANI 80	A = A AND 80
2008	RRC	Rotate A to Right without carry
2009	ANI 7F	A = A AND 7F
200B	XRA B	A = A XOR B
200C	DCR C	C = C – 1
200D	JNZ 2008	JUMP to 2008 if ZF = 0
2011	STA 3050	3050 <- A
2014	HLT	Stop

Explanation

1. LDA 2050 is used to load the data from address 2050 in A
2. MVI C, 07 is used to move the data 07 in C
3. MOV B, A moves the data of A to B
4. ANI 80 extracts the MSB(Most Significant Bit) of data available in A
5. RRC rotates the bits of A to right without carry
6. ANI 7F is used to take AND between data in A and 7F
7. XRA B takes XOR between the data present in A and B
8. DCR C is used to decrement the contents of C
9. JNZ 2008 is used to jump to address 2008 if ZF = 0
10. STA 3050 is used to store the result at memory address 3050
11. HLT is used to end the program

8085 program to convert 8 bit BCD number into ASCII Code

Problem

Write an assembly level language program to convert 8 bit BCD number to its respective ACSII Code.

Assumptions

Starting address of program: 2000
Input memory location: 2050
Output memory location: 3050 and 3051

Example

Input

Memory Address	2050
Input Data	98

Output

Memory Address	3050	3051
Output Data	38	39

ASCII Code for Digits 0 – 9

KEY	ASCII(HEX)	BINARY	BCD(UNPACKED)
0	30	011 0000	0000 0000
1	31	011 0001	0000 0001
2	32	011 0010	0000 0010
3	33	011 0011	0000 0011
4	34	011 0100	0000 0100
5	35	011 0101	0000 0101
6	36	011 0110	0000 0110
7	37	011 0111	0000 0111
8	38	011 1000	0000 1000
9	39	011 1001	0000 1001

Algorithm

1. Input the content of 2050 in accumulator
2. Move content of Accumulator to register B
3. Separate the least significant digit using AND with 0F and ADD 30 to accumulator
4. Store content of accumulator to memory location 3050
5. Move content of register B to Accumulator
6. Separate the most significant digit using AND with F0
7. Rotate Content of Accumulator 4 times
8. ADD 30 to accumulator
9. Store content of accumulator to memory location 3051

Program

Address	Mnemonics	Comment
2000	LDA 2050	A <- [2050]
2003	MOV B, A	B <- A

2004	ANI 0F	A <- A & 0F
2006	ADI 30	A <- A + 30
2008	STA 3050	[3050]<-A
200B	MOV A, B	A <- B
200C	ANI F0	A <- A & F0
200E	RLC	Rotate A left
200F	RLC	Rotate A left
2010	RLC	Rotate A left
2011	RLC	Rotate A left
2012	ADI 30	A <- A + 30
2014	STA 3051	[3051]<-A
2017	HLT	Stop Execution

Explanation

1. LDA 2050 load the content of memory location 2050 to accumulator
2. MOV B, A copy the content of accumulator to register B
3. ANI 0F AND the content of accumulator with immediate data 0F
4. ADI 30 ADD 30 to accumulator
5. STA 3050 store the content of accumulator to memory location 3050
6. MOV A, B copy the content of register B to accumulator
7. ANI F0 AND the content of accumulator with immediate data F0
8. RLC rotate the content of accumulator left without carry
9. RLC rotate the content of accumulator left without carry

10. RLC rotate the content of accumulator left without carry
11. RLC rotate the content of accumulator left without carry
12. ADI 30 ADD 30 to accumulator
13. STA 3051 store the content of accumulator to memory location 3051
14. HLT stops the execution of program

8085 code to convert binary number to ASCII code

Problem

Assembly level program in 8085 which converts a binary number into ASCII number.

Example

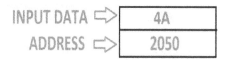

INPUT DATA ⇨ 4A
ADDRESS ⇨ 2050

OUTPUT DATA ⇨ 41 | 34
ADDRESS ⇨ 3050 | 3051

Assumptions

Binary number which have to convert in ASCII value is stored at memory location 2050 and output will be displayed at memory location 3050 and 3051.

Algorithm

1. Load the content of 2050.
2. Then separate the LSB of the no. using ANI 0F instruction and MSB of the number by again loading the content of 2050 and rotate it by one bit 4 times to get reverse of the number and then again use ANI 0F to separate the digit.
3. If the digit is more than or equal to 0A (in hexadecimal) then add 37 otherwise add 30 to convert into ASCII value (For checking the number is greater than or equal to A then use instruction: CPI 0A and then check the carry flag, if it is 0 then it means digit is greater than or equal to A and if 1 digit is less than A).
4. Now Store the ASCII values of both the digits in 3050 and 3051 respectively.

Program

Main routine:

Address	Mnemonics	Comment
2000	LDA 2050	A<-[2050]
2003	CALL 2500	go to address 2500
2006	STA 3050	A->[3050]
2009	LDA 2050	A<-[2050]
200C	RLC	Rotate the number by one bit to left without carry
200D	RLC	Rotate the number by one bit to left without carry
200E	RLC	Rotate the number by one bit to left without carry
200F	RLC	Rotate the number by one bit to left without carry
2010	CALL 2500	go to address 2500

| 2013 | STA 3051 | A->[3051] |
| 2016 | HLT | Terminates the program |

Sub routine

Address	Mnemonics	Comment
2500	ANI 0F	A<-[A] AND 0F
2502	CPI 0A	[A]-0A
2504	JNC 250A	Jump to [250A] if carry flag is 0
2507	ADI 30	A<-[A]+30
2509	RET	Return to the next instruction from where subroutine address was called in main routine
250A	ADI 37	A<-[A]+37
250C	RET	Return to the next instruction from where subroutine address was called in main routine

Explanation
Main routine:

1. LDA 2050: This instruction will load the number from address 2050 to the accumulator.
2. CALL 2500: This instruction will stop executing the main routine instructions after it and will move to the subroutine address 2500 for performing the subtask and after

performing subroutine instructions it will come back to main routine and execute the instructions after CALL 2500.

3. STA 3050: This instruction will store the result (performed in subroutine) of Accumulator to address 3050.

4. LDA 2050: This instruction will again load the number from address 2050 to the accumulator as the earlier loaded number is changed in accumulator.

5. RLC: Rotate the contents of Accumulator by one bit left side without carry.

6. RLC: Rotate the contents of Accumulator by one bit left side without carry.

7. RLC: Rotate the contents of Accumulator by one bit left side without carry.

8. RLC: Rotate the contents of Accumulator by one bit left side without carry.
(Applying RLC 4 times it will reverse the contents of the Accumulator)

9. CALL 2500: This instruction will stop executing the main routine instructions after it and will move to the subroutine address 2500 for performing the subtask and after performing subroutine instructions it will come back to main routine and execute the instructions after CALL 2500.

10. STA 3051: This instruction will store the result (performed in subroutine) of Accumulator to address 3051.

11. HLT: This instruction will terminate the program.

Sub routine

1. ANI 0F: This instruction will separate the LSB of the number present in Accumulator and stores the result back in Accumulator.

2. CPI 0A: This instruction will compare the content of Accumulator with 0A i.e. [A]-0A.

3. JNC 205A: If the carry flag becomes 0 then it will jump to 205A otherwise move to the next instruction.

4. ADI 30: It will add 30 to the content of Accumulator and again store the result back in Accumulator.

5. RET: Now it will move back to the main routine after the next instruction of CALL and start executing instructions of main routine.

6. ADI 37: It will add 37 to the content of Accumulator and again store the result back in Accumulator.
7. RET: Now it will move back to the main routine after the next instruction of CALL and start executing instructions of main routine.

8085 program to search a number in an array of n numbers

Problem

Write an assembly language program in 8085 to search a given number in an array of n numbers. If number is found, then store F0 in memory location 3051 otherwise store 0F in 3051.

Assumptions

Count of elements in an array is stored at memory location 2050. Array is stored from starting memory address 2051 and number which user want to search is stored at memory location 3050.

Examples

DATA ⇨	04	49	F2	14	39
ADDRESS ⇨	2050	2051	2052	2053	2054

OUTPUT
⇩

DATA ⇨	F2	F0
ADDRESS ⇨	3050	3051

DATA	04	49	F2	14	39
ADDRESS	2050	2051	2052	2053	2054

OUTPUT
⇩

DATA	17	0F
ADDRESS	3050	3051

Algorithm

1. Make the memory pointer points to memory location 2050 by help of LXI H 2050 instruction
2. Store value of array size in register C
3. Store number to be search in register B
4. Increment memory pointer by 1 so that it points to next array index
5. Store element of array in accumulator A and compare it with value of B
6. If both are same i.e. if ZF = 1 then store F0 in A and store the result in memory location 3051 and go to step 9
7. Otherwise store 0F in A and store it in memory location 3051
8. Decrement C by 01 and check if C is not equal to zero i.e. ZF = 0, if true go to step 3 otherwise go to step 9
9. End of program

Program

Address	Mnemonics	Comment
2000	LXI H 2050	H <- 20, L <- 50
2003	MOV C, M	C <- M
2004	LDA 3050	A <- M[3050]

2007	MOV B, A	B <- A
2008	INX H	HL <- HL + 0001
2009	MOV A, M	A <- M
200A	CMP B	A – B
200B	JNZ 2014	Jump if ZF = 0
200E	MVI A F0	A <- F0
2010	STA 3051	M[3051] <- A
2013	HLT	END
2014	MVI A 0F	A <- 0F
2016	STA 3051	M[3051] <- A
2019	DCR C	C <- C – 01
201A	JNZ 2008	Jump if ZF = 0
201D	HLT	END

Explanation

Registers used A, B, C, H, L and indirect memory M:
1. LXI H 2050: initialize register H with 20 and register L with 50
2. MOV C, M: assign content of indirect memory location, M which is represented by registers H and L to register C
3. LDA 3050: loads the content of memory location 3050 in accumulator A
4. MOV B, A: move the content of A in register B
5. INX H: increment HL by 1, i.e. M is incremented by 1 and now M will point to next memory location
6. MOV A, M: move the content of memory location M in accumulator A

7. CMP B: subtract B from A and update flags of 8085
8. JNZ 2014: jump to memory location 2014 if zero flag is reset i.e. ZF = 0
9. MVI A F0: assign F0 to A
10. STA 3051: stores value of A in 3051
11. HLT: stops executing the program and halts any further execution
12. MVI A 0F: assign 0F to A
13. STA 3051: stores value of A in 3051
14. DCR C: decrement C by 01
15. JNZ 2008: jump to memory location 2008 if zero flag is reset
16. HLT: stops executing the program and halts any further execution

8085 program for Linear search | Set 2

Problem

Write an assembly language program in 8085 microprocessor to find a given number in the list of 10 numbers, if found store 1 in output else store 0 in output.

Example

List :	42H	21H	01H	1FH	FFH	25H	32H	34H	0AH	ABH

Data: 25H   Output: 01H

Assumption

Data to be found at 2040H, list of numbers from 2050H to 2059H and output at 2060H.

Algorithm

1. Load data byte to be searched in B register and counter in D register.
2. Load starting element in Accumulator.

3. Compare Accumulator and B register.
4. If zero flag is set then JUMP to point 8 (as CMP instruction sets Zero flag when both are equal).
5. Decrement D register
6. If D>0 take next element in Accumulator and go to point 3.
7. If D=0, this means element not found then store 00H. End the program.
8. Store 01H as element found. End the program.

Program

Address	Label	Mnemonics	Comment
2000H	Data	LXI H, 2040H	Load address of data to be searched
2003H		MOV B, M	Store data to be searched in B register
2004H		LXI H, 2050H	Load starting address of list
2007H		MVI D, 0AH	Counter for 10 elements
2009H	NEXT	MOV A, M	Retrieve list element in Accumulator
200AH		CMP B	Compare element with data byte
200BH		JZ STOP	Jump if data byte found
200EH		INX H	Next element of list
200FH		DCR D	Decrement counter
2010H		JNZ NEXT	Jump to NEXT if D>0
2013H		LXI H, 2060H	Load address of output
2016H		MVI M, 00H	Store 00H
2018H		HLT	Halt
2019H	STOP	LXI H, 2060H	Load address of output
201CH		MVI M, 01H	Store 01H
201EH		HLT	Halt

1. One by one all elements are compared with data byte in B register
2. If element found, loop ends and 01H is stored
3. Loop executes 10 number of times
4. If at the end of 10 iterations, data byte is not found then 00H is stored

8085 program to find largest number in an array

Problem

Determine largest number in an array of n elements. Value of n is stored at address 2050 and array starts from address 2051. Result is stored at address 3050. Starting address of program is taken as 2000.

Example

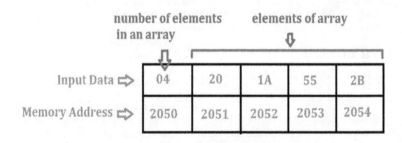

	number of elements in an array	elements of array			
Input Data ⇨	04	20	1A	55	2B
Memory Address ⇨	2050	2051	2052	2053	2054

largest element

Output Data ⇨	55
Memory Address ⇨	3050

Algorithm

1. We are taking first element of array in A
2. Comparing A with other elements of array, if A is smaller than store that element in A otherwise compare with next element
3. The value of A is the answer

Program

Address	Mnemonics	Comment
2000	LXI H 2050	H←20, L←50
2003	MOV C, M	C←M
2004	DCR C	C←C-01
2005	INX H	HL←HL+0001
2006	MOV A, M	A←M
2007	INX H	HL←HL+0001
2008	CMP M	A-M
2009	JNC 200D	If Carry Flag=0, goto 200D
200C	MOV A, M	A←M
200D	DCR C	C←C-1
200E	JNZ 2007	If Zero Flag=0, goto 2007
2011	STA 3050	A→3050
2014	HLT	

Explanation

Registers used: A, H, L, C
1. LXI 2050 assigns 20 to H and 50 to L
2. MOV C, M copies content of memory (specified by HL register pair) to C (this is used as a counter)
3. DCR C decrements value of C by 1
4. INX H increases value of HL by 1. This is done to visit next memory location
5. MOV A, M copies content of memory (specified by HL register pair) to A
6. INX H increases value of HL by 1. This is done to visit next memory location
7. CMP M compares A and M by subtracting M from A. Carry flag and sign flag becomes set if A-M is negative
8. JNC 200D jumps program counter to 200D if carry flag = 0
9. MOV A, M copies content of memory (specified by HL register pair) to A
10. DCR C decrements value of C by 1
11. JNZ 2007 jumps program counter to 2007 if zero flag = 0
12. STA 3050 stores value of A at 3050 memory location
13. HLT stops executing the program and halts any further execution

8085 program for bubble sort

Problem
Write an assembly language program in 8085 microprocessor to sort a given list of n numbers using Bubble Sort.

Example

		List				
Size	INPUT:	35H	10H	02H	21H	F0H
05H						
		List				
	OUTPUT:	02H	10H	21H	35H	F0H

Assumption

Size of list is stored at 2040H and list of numbers from 2041H onwards.

Algorithm

1. Load size of list in C register and set D register to be 0
2. Decrement C as for n elements n-1 comparisons occur
3. Load the starting element of the list in Accumulator
4. Compare Accumulator and next element
5. If accumulator is less than next element jump to step 8
6. Swap the two elements
7. Set D register to 1
8. Decrement C
9. If C>0 take next element in Accumulator and go to point 4
10. If D=0, this means in the iteration, no exchange takes place consequently we know that it won't take place in further iterations so the loop in exited and program is stopped
11. Jump to step 1 for further iterations

Program

Address	Label	Mnemonics	Comment
2000H	START	LXI H, 2040H	Load size of array
2003H		MVI D, 00H	Clear D register to set up a flag
2005H		MOV C, M	Set C register with number of elements in list

2006H		DCR C	Decrement C
2007H		INX H	Increment memory to access list
2008H	CHECK	MOV A, M	Retrieve list element in Accumulator
2009H		INX H	Increment memory to access next element
200AH		CMP M	Compare Accumulator with next element
200BH		JC NEXTBYTE	If accumulator is less then jump to NEXTBYTE
200EH		MOV B, M	Swap the two elements
200FH		MOV M, A	
2010H		DCX H	
2011H		MOV M, B	
2012H		INX H	
2013H		MVI D, 01H	If exchange occurs save 01 in D register
2015H	NEXTBYTE	DCR C	Decrement C for next iteration
2016H		JNZ CHECK	Jump to CHECK if C>0
2019H		MOV A, D	Transfer contents of D to Accumulator
201AH		CPI 01H	Compare accumulator contents with 01H
201CH		JZ START	Jump to START if D=01H
201FH		HLT	HALT

- Retrieve an element in accumulator.
- Compare it with next element, if it is greater, then swap otherwise move to next index.
- If in one entire loop there has been no exchange, halt otherwise start the whole iteration again.
- The following approach has two loops, one nested inside other so-
  Worst and Average Case Time Complexity: O(n*n). Worst case occurs when array is reverse sorted.
  Best Case Time Complexity: O(n). Best case occurs when array is already sorted.

8085 program to swap two 8-bit numbers

Problem

Write an assembly language program to swap two 8-bit numbers stored in 8085 microprocessor.

Assumption

Suppose there are two 8-bit numbers. One 8-bit number is stored at location 2500 memory address and another is stored at location 2501 memory address. Let 05 is stored at location 2500 and 06 is stored at location 2501 (not necessarily, can be any two 8-bit numbers).

Example

INPUT	
ADDRESS	**DATA**
2500	05
2501	06

OUTPUT	
ADDRESS	**DATA**
2500	06 ←
2501	05 ← Swapped

Algorithm

1. Load accumulator with the content of any one location (either 2500 or 2501 or any given location).
2. Move the contents of accumulator to any register (say B) so that another location's content can be loaded to accumulator and the previous data of accumulator get saved in register.
3. Store the content of accumulator to another location (data of 2501 to 2500).
4. Load accumulator with content of register and then store it to another address location.

Program

Address	Mnemonics	Comment
2000	LDA 2500	A<-[2500]
2003	MOV B,A	B<-A
2004	LDA 2501	A<-[2501]
2007	STA 2500	2500<-[A]

200A	MOV A,B	A<-B
200B	STA 2501	2501<-[A]
200E	HLT	Terminates the program

1. LDA 2500: Load accumulator with content of location 2500
2. MOV B,A: Copy content of accumulator to register B
3. LDA 2501: Load accumulator with content of location 2501
4. STA 2500: Store content of accumulator to location 2500
5. MOV A,B: Copy content of register B to accumulator
6. STA 2501: Store content of accumulator to location 2501
7. HLT: Terminates the program

8085 program to swap two 8 bit numbers using Direct addressing mode

Problem

Write a program to swap two 8-bit numbers using direct addressing mode where starting address is 2000 and the first 8-bit number is stored at 3000 and the second 8-bit number is stored at 3001 memory address.

Example

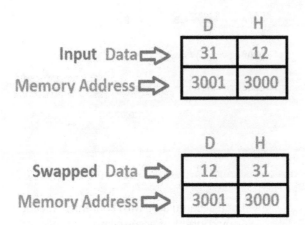

	D	H
Input Data ⇒	31	12
Memory Address ⇒	3001	3000

	D	H
Swapped Data ⇒	12	31
Memory Address ⇒	3001	3000

Algorithm

1. Load a 8-bit number from memory 3000 into accumulator
2. Move value of accumulator into register H
3. Load a 8-bit number from memory 3001 into accumulator
4. Move value of accumulator into register D
5. Exchange both the register pairs
6. Stop

Program

Address	Mnemonics	Operands	Comment
2000	LDA	[3000]	[A] <- [3000]
2003	MOV	H, A	[H] <- [A]
2004	LDA	[3001]	[A] <- [3001]
2007	MOV	D, A	[D] <- [A]
2008	XCHG		[H-L] [D-E]
2009	HLT		Stop

Registers A, H, D are used for general purpose.
1. LDA is used to load accumulator direct using 16-bit address (3 Byte instruction)
2. MOV is used to transfer the data (1 Byte instruction)
3. XCHG is used to exchange the data of both the register pair (H-L), (D-E) (1 Byte instruction)
4. HLT is used to halt the program.

8085 program to swap two 16 bit numbers using Direct addressing mode

Problem
Write a program to swap two 16-bit numbers using direct addressing mode where starting address is 2000 and the first 16-bit number is stored at 3000 and the second 16-bit number is stored at 3002 memory address.
Example

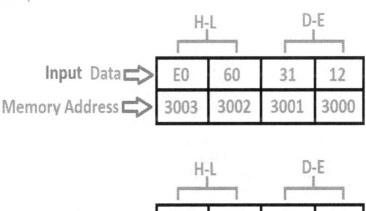

Algorithm

1. Load a 16-bit number from memory 3000 into a register pair (H-L)
2. Exchange the register pairs
3. Load a 16-bit number from memory 3002 into a register pair (H-L)
4. Exchange both the register pairs
5. Stop

Program

Address	Mnemonics	Operands	Comment
2000	LHLD	[3000]	[H-L] <- [3000]
2003	XCHG		[H-L] [D-E]
2004	LHLD	[3002]	[H-L] <- [3002]
2007	XCHG		[H-L] [D-E]
2008	HLT		Stop

Explanation

Registers (H-L) pair, (D-E) pair are used for general purpose.
1. LHLD is used to load register pair H-L direct using 16-bit address (3 Byte instruction)
2. XCHG is used to exchange the data of both the register pair (H-L), (D-E) (1 Byte instruction)
3. HLT is used to halt the program.

8085 program to exchange a block of bytes in memory

Problem

Write an assembly level program in 8085 microprocessor to exchange a block of 4 bytes staring from address 2001 with data starting from address 3001.

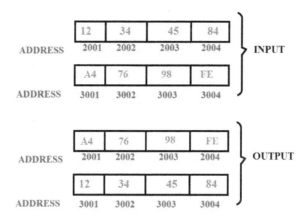

Algorithm

1. Take a count equal to 4
2. Store the starting address of both blocks in 2 different register pairs
3. Now exchange the contents at the addresses in both register pairs
4. Increment the values of both register pairs
5. Decrements count by 1
6. If count is not equal to 0 repeat steps 3 to 5

Program

Address	Mnemonics	Comment
2500	LXI D 2001	D <= 20, E <= 01
2503	LXI H 3001	H <= 20, L <= 01

2506	MVI C 04	C <= 04
2508	MOV B, M	B <= M[H-L]
2509	LDAX D	A <= M[D-E]
250A	MOV M, A	M[H-L] <= A
250B	MOV A, B	A <= B
250C	STAX D	M[D-E] <= A
250D	INX H	[H-L] <= [H-L] + 1
250E	INX D	[D-E] <= [D-E] + 1
250F	DCR C	C <= C – 1
2510	JNZ 2508	JUMP TO 2508 IF C NOT EQUAL TO 0
2513	HLT	STOP THE PROGRAM

Explanation

1. LXI D 2001: Loads register pair, that is in this case, D=20 and E=01
   LXI H 3001 – H=30 and L=01
2. MVI C 04: Assigns immediate data. E.g. here C=04
   MVI A 45: assigns A(accumulator) with 45, A=45
3. MOV B, M: Here M is the data in H – L register pair and it serves as an address. Copies content at address stored in M to register B
4. LDAX D: Here Accumulator is loaded with the data stored at address formed by register pair D – E
5. MOV M, A: Here A's content is copied to address which is stored in M.
   MOV A, B: Copies content of register B to A

6. STAX D: Stores the content of A (accumulator) in the address formed by register pair D – E.
7. INX H: Increment the content of register pair H – L
8. INX H: Increment the content of register pair D – E
9. DCR C: Decrements the content of register C
10. JNZ 2508: If value of register C is not equal to 0 then jump to address 2508
11. HLT: Stop execution of program

8085 program to access and exchange the content of Flag register with register B

Problem

Write an assembly language program in 8085 microprocessor to access Flag register and exchange the content of flag register F with register B.

Example

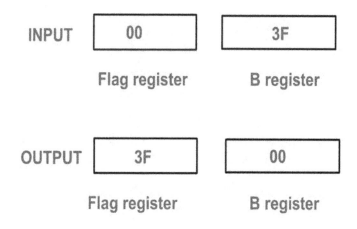

INPUT   00   3F

Flag register   B register

OUTPUT   3F   00

Flag register   B register

Assumptions

Initial values of flag register, register B and stack pointer are is 00, 3F, and 3FFF respectively.

PSW stands for PROGRAM STATUS WORD. PSW combines accumulator A and flag register F.

Algorithm

1. Push the value of PSW in memory stack by help of PUSH instruction
2. Pop the value of Flag register and store it in register H by help of POP instruction
3. Move the value of register H in register C
4. Move the value of register B in register H
5. Move the value of register C in register B
6. Push the value of register H in memory stack by help of PUSH instruction
7. Pop the value of PSW from memory stack using POP instruction

Program

Address	Mnemonics	Comment
2000	PUSH PSW	Push value of accumulator and flag in stack
2001	POP H	Pop value from TOP of memory stack in H
2002	MOV C, H	C <- H
2003	MOV H, B	H <- B
2004	MOV B, C	B <- C
2005	PUSH H	Push the value of register H
2006	POP PSW	Pop value of flag register and Accumulator

2007	HLT	END	

Explanation

Registers used A, B, C, H, F

1. PUSH PSW instruction performs the following task:
   SP <- SP – 1
   M[SP] <- A
   SP <- SP – 1
   M[SP] <- F
2. POP H instruction performs the following task:
   H <- M[SP]
   SP <- SP + 1
3. MOV C, H: moves the value of H in register C
4. MOV H, B: moves the value of B in register H, hence H is updated
5. MOV B, C: moves the value of C in register B, hence B is updated
6. PUSH H performs the following task:
   SP <- SP – 1
   M[SP] <- H
7. POP PSW performs the following task:
   F <- M[SP]
   SP <- SP + 1
   A <- M[SP]
   SP <- SP + 1
8. HLT: stops executing the program and halts any further execution

8085 program to exchange content of HL register pair with DE register pair

Problem

Write an assembly language program in 8085 microprocessor to exchange content of HL register pair with DE register pair using PUSH and POP instructions.

Example

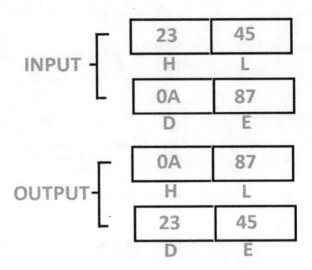

Assumption

Content is already present in HL and DE register.

Algorithm

1. Initialize stack pointer (SP) by 3FFF.
2. Push the content of H and L register into the stack. Decrements SP by 2.
3. Push the content of D and E register into the stack. Decrements SP by 2.
4. Pop the upper two bytes from top of stack and place it in HL register. Increment SP by 2.
5. Pop the remaining two bytes from top of stack and place it in DE register. Increment SP by 2.

Program

Address	Mnemonics	Comment
2000	LXI SP 3FFF	SP <- 3FFF
2003	PUSH H	SP <- SP – 1, M[SP] <- H, SP <- SP – 1, M[SP] <- L
2004	PUSH D	SP <- SP – 1, M[SP] <- D, SP <- SP – 1, M[SP] <- E
2005	POP H	L <- M[SP], SP <- SP + 1, H <- M[SP], SP <- SP + 1
2006	POP D	E <- M[SP], SP <- SP + 1, D <- M[SP], SP <- SP + 1
2007	HLT	ENDT

Explanation

Registers used H, L, D, E:
1. LXI SP 3FFF: initialize SP by 3FFF.
2. PUSH H: push the content of H and L register into the stack and decrements stack pointer by 2.
3. PUSH D: push the content of D and E register into the stack and decrements stack pointer by 2.
4. POP H: pop the upper two bytes from top of stack and place it in HL register pair and increment SP by 2.
5. POP D: pop the upper two bytes from top of stack and place it in DE register pair and increment SP by 2.
6. HLT: stops executing the program and halts any further execution.

8085 program to move blocks of bits from source location to a destination location

Problem

Write a program to move blocks of bits from source location starting at **2500** to destination location starting from **2600** where size of blocks is **05** bytes.

Input Data ⇨	05	04	03	02	01
Memory Address ⇨	2504	2503	2502	2501	2500

Moved Data

Output Data ⇨	05	04	03	02	01
Memory Address ⇨	2604	2603	2602	2601	2600

Algorithm

1. Load register pair H-L with the address 2500H
2. Load register pair D-E with the address 2600H
3. Move the content at memory location into accumulator
4. Store the content of accumulator into memory pointed by D-E
5. Increment value of register pair H-L and D-E by 1
6. Decrements value of register C by 1
7. If zero flag not equal to 1, go to step 3
8. Stop

Program

Address	Mnemonics	Operands	Comment
2000	MVI	C, 05	[C] <- 05
2002	LXI	H, 2500	[H-L] <- 2500
2005	LXI	D, 2600	[D-E] <- 2600

2008	MOV	A, M	[A] <- [[H-L]]
2009	STAX	D	[A] -> [[D-E]]
200A	INX	H	[H-L] <- [H-L] + 1
200B	INX	D	[D-E] <- [D-E] + 1
200C	DCR	C	[C] <- [C] – 1
200D	JNZ	2008	Jump if not zero to 2008
2010	HLT		Stop

Explanation

Registers A, D, E, H, L, C are used for general purpose:
1. MOV is used to transfer the data from memory to accumulator (1 Byte)
2. LXI is used to load register pair immediately using 16-bit address (3 Byte instruction)
3. MVI is used to move data immediately into any of registers (2 Byte)
4. STAX is used to store accumulator into register pair indirectly (3 Byte instruction)
5. DCR is used to decrease register by 1 (1 Byte instruction)
6. INX is used to increase register pair by 1 (1 Byte instruction)
7. JNZ is used to jump if not zero to given memory location (3 Byte instruction)
8. HLT is used to halt the program

8085 program to generate Fibonacci series

Problem

Write an assembly language program in 8085 microprocessor to generate Fibonacci series.

Example

Assume Fibonacci series is stored at starting memory location 3050.

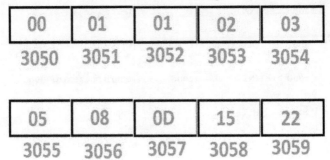

00	01	01	02	03
3050	3051	3052	3053	3054

05	08	0D	15	22
3055	3056	3057	3058	3059

Note: This program generates Fibonacci series in hexadecimal numbers.

Algorithm

1. Initialize register H with 30 and register L with 50, so that indirect memory M points to memory location 3050.
2. Initialize register B with 00, register C with 08 and register D with 01.
3. Move the content of B in M.
4. Increment M by 1 so that M points to next memory location.
5. Move the content of D in M.
6. Move the content of B in accumulator A.
7. Add the content of D in A.
8. Move the content of D in B.
9. Move the content of A in D.
10. Increment M by 1 so that M points to next memory location.
11. Move the content of A in M.
12. Decrements C by 1.
13. Jump to memory location 200C if ZF = 0 otherwise Halt the program.

Address	Mnemonics	Comment
2000	LXI H, 3050	H <- 30, L <- 50
2003	MVI C, 08	C <- 08
2005	MVI B, 00	B <- 00
2007	MVI D, 01	D <- 01
2009	MOV M, B	M <- B
200A	INX H	M <- M + 01
200B	MOV M, D	M <- D
200C	MOV A, B	A <- B
200C	ADD D	A <- A + D
200E	MOV B, D	B <- D
200F	MOV D, A	D <- A
2010	INX H	M <- M + 01
2011	MOV M, A	M <- A
2012	DCR C	C <- C - 01
2013	JNZ 200C	Jump if ZF = 0
2016	HLT	END

Explanation

Registers A, B, C, D, H, L are used for general purpose.
1. LXI H 3050: assigns 30 to H and 50 to L.
2. MVI B, 00: assigns 00 to B.
3. MVI C, 08: assigns 08 to C.
4. MVI D, 01: assigns 01 to D.
5. MOV M, B: moves the content of B in M.
6. INX H: increment M by 1.

7. MOV M, D: moves the content of D in M.
8. MOV A, B: moves the content of B in A.
9. ADD D: add the content of D and A. Store the result in A.
10. MOV B, D: moves the content of D in B.
11. MOV D, A: moves the content of A in D.
12. INX H: increment M by 1.
13. MOV M, A: moves the content of A in M.
14. DCR C: decrements C by 1.
15. JNZ 200C: jump to memory location 200C if ZF = 0.
16. HLT: stops executing the program and halts any further execution.

8085 program to show masking of lower and higher nibbles of 8 bit number

Problem

Write an assembly language program in 8085 microprocessor to show masking of lower and higher nibble of 8 bit number.

Example

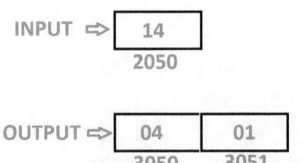

Assumption

8 bit number is stored at memory location 2050. After masking of nibbles, lower order nibble is stored at memory location 3050 and higher order nibble is stored at memory location 3051.

1. Load the content of memory location 2050 in accumulator A.
2. Move the content of A in register B.
3. Perform AND operation of A with 0F and store the result in memory location 3050.
4. Move the content of B in A.
5. Perform AND operation of A with 0F and reverse the result by using **RLC** instruction 4 times.
6. Store the result in memory location 3051.

Program

Address	Mnemonics	Comment
2000	LDA 2050	A <- M[2050]
2003	MOV B, A	B <- A
2004	ANI 0F	A <- A (AND) 0F
2006	STA 3050	M[3050] <- A
2009	MOV A, B	A <- B
200A	ANI 0F	A <- A (AND) 0F
200C	RLC	rotate content of A left by 1 bit without carry
200D	RLC	rotate content of A left by 1 bit without carry
200E	RLC	rotate content of A left by 1 bit without carry
200F	RLC	rotate content of A left by 1 bit without carry

2010	STA 3051	M[3051] <- A
2013	HLT	END

Registers A, B are used:
1. LDA 2050: load the content of memory location 2050 in accumulator A.
2. MOV B, A: moves the content of A to B.
3. ANI 0F: perform AND operation of A with 0F and store the result back to A.
4. STA 3050: store content of A in memory location 3050.
5. MOV A, B: moves the content of B in A.
6. ANI 0F: perform AND operation of A with 0F and store the result back to A.
7. RLC: rotate content of A left by 1 bit without carry. Use this instruction 4 times to reverse the content of A.
8. STA 3051: store the content of A in memory location 3051.
9. HLT: stops executing the program and halts any further execution.

8085 program to check whether the given 16 bit number is palindrome or not

Problem
Write an assembly language program to check whether the given 16 bit number is palindrome or not. If number is palindrome then store 01 at memory location 3050 otherwise store FF at memory location 3050.

Note: A palindrome number is a number that remains the same when its digits are reversed.

Assume that 16 bit number, to check for palindrome is stored at memory location 2050.

Examples

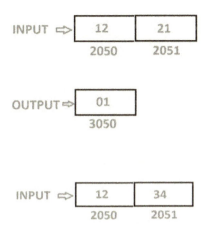

INPUT ⇨ | 12 | 21 |
|---|---|
| 2050 | 2051 |

OUTPUT ⇨ | 01 |
|---|
| 3050 |

INPUT ⇨ | 12 | 34 |
|---|---|
| 2050 | 2051 |

OUTPUT ⇨ | FF |
|---|
| 3050 |

Algorithm

1. Load contents of memory location 2050 in register L and contents of memory location 2051 in register H
2. Move contents of L in accumulator A
3. Reverse the contents of A by executing RLC instruction 4 times
4. Move the contents of A in L
5. Move the contents of H in A
6. Reverse the contents of A by executing RLC instruction 4 times
7. Move the contents of L in H
8. Move the contents of A in L
9. Store the content of L in memory location 2070 and contents of H in memory location 2071
10. Load the content of memory location 2050 in A
11. Move the content of A in register B
12. Load the content of memory location 2070 in A
13. Compare content of A and B. If the content is not same then store FF in A and store it in memory location 3050

14. If contents of A and B are same, then Load the content of memory location 2051 in A
15. Move the content of A in B
16. Load the content of memory location 2071 in A
17. Compare content of A and B. If the content is not same then store FF in A and store it in memory location 3050
18. If contents of A and B are same, then store 01 in A and store it in memory location 3050

Program

Address	Mnemonics	Comment
2000	LHLD 2050	L <- M[2050], H <- M[2051]
2003	MOV A, L	A <- L
2004	RLC	Rotate accumulator content left by 1 bit without carry
2005	RLC	Rotate accumulator content left by 1 bit without carry
2006	RLC	Rotate accumulator content left by 1 bit without carry
2007	RLC	Rotate accumulator content left by 1 bit without carry
2008	MOV L, A	L <- A
2009	MOV A, H	A <- H
200A	RLC	Rotate accumulator content left by 1 bit without carry
200B	RLC	Rotate accumulator content left by 1 bit without carry
200C	RLC	Rotate accumulator content left by 1 bit without carry
200D	RLC	Rotate accumulator content left by 1 bit without carry
200E	MOV H, L	H <- L

200F	MOV L, A	L <- A
2010	SHLD 2070	M[2070] <- L, M[2071] <- H
2013	LDA 2050	A <- M[2050]
2016	MOV B, A	B <- A
2017	LDA 2070	A <- M[2070]
201A	CMP B	A – B
201B	JZ 2024	Jump if ZF = 0
201E	MVI A, FF	A <- 01
2020	STA 3050	M[3050] <- A
2023	HLT	END
2024	LDA 2051	A <- M[2051]
2027	MOV B, A	B <- A
2028	LDA 2071	A <- M[2071]
202B	CMP B	A – B
202C	JZ 2035	Jump if ZF = 0
202F	MVI A, FF	A <- FF
2031	STA 3050	M[3050] <- A
2034	HLT	END
2035	MVI A, 01	A <- 01

2037	STA 3050	M[3050] <- A
203A	HLT	END

Explanation

Registers A, H, L, B are used for general purpose.

1. LHLD 2050: loads contents of memory location 2050 in L and 2051 in H.
2. MOV A, L: moves content of L in A.
3. RLC: shift the content of A left by one bit without carry. Repeat the current instruction 4 times so that contents of A get reversed.
4. MOV L, A: moves the content of A in L.
5. MOV A, H: moves the content of H in A.
6. RLC: shift the content of A left by one bit without carry. Repeat the current instruction 4 times so that contents of A get reversed.
7. MOV H, L: moves the content of L in H.
8. MOV L, A: moves the content of A in L.
9. SHLD 2070: stores the content of L in 2070 and H in 2071.
10. LDA 2050: load the content of memory location 2050 in A.
11. MOV B, A: moves the content of A in B.
12. CMP B: compares the content of A and B. It set the zero flag if content is same otherwise reset.
13. JZ 2024: jump to memory location 2024 if ZF = 1.
14. MVI A, FF: store FF in A.
15. STA 3050: store content of A in 3050.
16. HLT: stops executing the program and halts any further execution.
17. LDA 2051: load the content of memory location 2050 in A.
18. MOV B, A: moves the content of A in B.
19. LDA 2071: load the content of memory location 2071 in A.
20. CMP B: compares the content of A and B. It set the zero flag if content is same otherwise reset.
21. JZ 2035: jump to memory location 2035 if ZF = 1.
22. MVI A, FF: store FF in A.
23. STA 3050: store content of A in 3050.

24. **HLT:** stops executing the program and halts any further execution.
25. **MVI A, 01:** store 01 in A.
26. **STA 3050:** store content of A in 3050.
27. **HLT:** stops executing the program and halts any further execution.

8085 program to transfer the status of switches

Problem

Write an assembly language program in 8085 of interfacing between 8085 and 8255. 8 switches are connected at port A. Transfer the status of these switches into port B where LEDs are connected.

Example

D7	D6	D5	D4	D3	D2	D1	D0
1	0	0	1	0	0	0	0

9   0

Input port is A and Output port is B.

Algorithm

1. Construct the control word register
2. Input the data from port A
3. Display the result in port B

Program

Mnemonics	Comment
MVI A, 90	A ← 92
OUT 83	Control Register ← A
IN 80	A → Port A;

OUT 81	Port C A ← A
RET	Return

Explanation

1. MVI A, 92 means that the value of control register is 92.
2. D7=1 as it is in I/O mode
3. D6=0 & D5=0 as Poet A is in mo mode
4. D4=1 as Port A is taking input
5. D3=0 & D0=0 as Port C is not taking part
6. D2=0 as mode of Port B is mo
   D1=0 as Port B is displaying the result
7. OUT 83 putting the value of A in 83H which is the port number of port control register.
8. IN 80 taking input from 80H which is the port number of port A.
9. OUT 81 displaying the result in 81H which is the port number of port B.
10. RET return

8085 program to interface 8255 for addition

Problem
Interface 8255 with 8085 microprocessor and write an assembly program which determine the addition of contents of port A and port B and store the result in port C.

Example

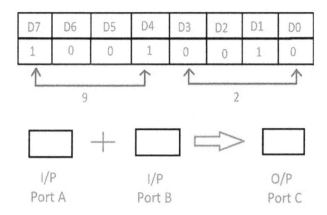

D7	D6	D5	D4	D3	D2	D1	D0
1	0	0	1	0	0	1	0

9   2

□ + □ ⇒ □

I/P Port A   I/P Port B   O/P Port C

Algorithm

1. Construct the control word register
2. Input the data from port A and port B
3. Add the contents of port A and port B
4. Display the result in port C

Program

Mnemonics	Comment
MVI A, 90	A ← 92
OUT 83	Control Register ← A
IN 80	A ← Port A;
MOV B, A	B ← A;
IN 81	A ← Port B;
ADD B	A ← A+B;
OUT 82	Port C ← A
RET	Return

Explanation
1. MVI A, 92 means that the value of control register is 92.
2. D7=1 as it is in I/O mode.
3. D6=0 & D5=0 as Poet A is in mo mode.
4. D4=1 as Port A is taking input.
5. D3=0 & D0=0 as Port C is not taking part.
6. D2=0 as mode of Port B is mo.
   D1=1 as Port B is taking the input.
7. OUT 83 putting the value of A in 83H which is the port number of port control register.
8. IN 80 taking input from 80H which is the port number of port A.
9. MOV B, A copies the content of A register to B register.
10. IN 81 take input from 81H which is the port number of port B.
11. ADD B add the contents of A register and B register.
12. OUT 82 displaying the result in 81H which is the port number of port C.
13. RET return

8085 program to interface 8255 for subtraction

Problem

Write an assembly program which determine the subtraction of contents of port B from port A and store the result in port C by interfacing 8255 with 8085 microprocessor.

Example

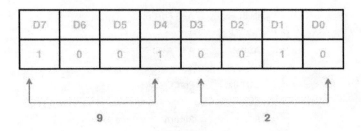

D7	D6	D5	D4	D3	D2	D1	D0
1	0	0	1	0	0	1	0

9   2

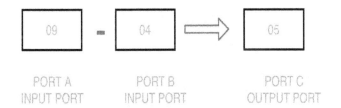

09	− 04	⇒ 05
PORT A	PORT B	PORT C
INPUT PORT	INPUT PORT	OUTPUT PORT

Algorithm

1. Construct the control word register
2. Input the data from port A and port B
3. Subtract the contents of port A and port B
4. Display the result in port C
5. Halt the program

Program

Mnemonics	Comment
MVI A, 92	A <- 92
OUT 83	Control Register <- A
IN 81	A <- Port B
MOV B, A	B <- A
IN 80	A <- Port A
SUB B	A <- A – B
OUT 82	Port C <- A
RET	Return

Explanation

1. MVI A, 92: means that the value of control register is 92.

2. D7=1: I/O mode
3. D6=0 & D5=0: Port A is in mode 0
4. D4=1: Port A is taking input
5. D3=0 & D0=0: Port C is not taking part
6. D2=0: Port B is in mode 0
7. D1=1: Port B is taking input
8. OUT 83: putting the value of A in 83H which is the port number of port control register.
9. IN 81: take input from 81H which is the port number of port B.
10. MOV B, A: copies the content of A register to B register.
11. IN 80: taking input from 80H which is the port number of port A.
12. SUB B: subtract the contents of A register and B register.
13. OUT 82: display the result in 81H which is the port number of port C.
14. RET: return

8085 program to print the table of input integer

Problem

Write an assembly language program in 8085 to print the table of input integer.

Assumption

Suppose the inputted number is at memory location 2050 and the table will be printed from starting location 3050.
Example

Input Data		02
Memory Address		2050

Output Data		02	04	06	08	0A
Memory Address		3050	3051	3052	3053	3054
Output Data		0C	0E	10	12	14
Memory Address		3055	3056	3057	3058	3059

Algorithm

1. Load the value of input in accumulator from memory location 2050 and then copy it to another register say D. Also store 0A in register B.
2. Store memory location 3050 in M using LXI instruction and take another register say C with its value 00.
3. Now copy the content of D register to A and add the contents of A and C and store it in A then copy it to M.
4. Increment value of M by 1.
5. Copy content of A to C and decrements the content of B by 1 and if its value is 0 then halt otherwise again go to step number 3.

Program

Address	Mnemonics	Comment
2000	LDA 2050	A<-[2050]
2003	MOV D, A	D<-[A]
2004	MVI B 0A	B<-0A

2006	LXI H 3050	H<-30 & L<-50
2009	MVI C 00	C<-00
200B	MOV A, D	A<-[D]
200C	ADD C	A<-[A]+[C]
200D	MOV M, A	M<-[A]
200E	INX H	HL<-HL+1
200F	MOV C, A	C<-[A]
2010	DCR B	B<-[B]-1
2011	JNZ 200B	Jump to address 200B if ZF=0
2014	HLT	Terminates the program

Explanation

1. LDA 2050: load the contents from 2050 memory location to accumulator (register A).
2. MOV D, A: move the contents of accumulator to register D.
3. MVI B 0A: store 0A data into register B.
4. LXI H 3050: store 30 in H register and 50 in L register, hence M will contain 3050 inside it.
5. MVI C 00: store 00 data in register C.
6. MOV A, D: move the contents of D register into A.
7. ADD C: add the contents of A and C register and store in A.
8. MOV M, A: move the contents of A register into M.
9. INX H: increments content of M by 1.
10. MOV C, A: move the contents of A register into C.
11. DCR B: decrements the content of B register by 1.
12. JNZ 200B: jump to address 200B if Carry flag is not zero.
13. HLT: terminate the program.

Write a program to count continuously in hexadecimal from FFH to 00H in a system with clock frequency 0.5 microseconds. Use register C to set up a delay of 1ms between each count and display output at one of the output ports.

Problem Analysis

1. The hexadecimal counter is set by loading a register with starting number and decrementing it till zero is reached and then again decrementing it to will produce -1, which is two's complement of FFH. Hence, the register again reaches FFH.
2. The 1ms time delay is set up by the procedure shown in flowchart-

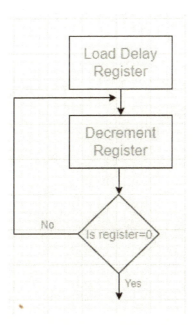

The register is loaded with appropriate number such that the execution of above loop produces a time delay of 1ms.

Program

Address	Label	Mnemonics
2000H		MVI B, FFH
2002H	NEXT	DCR B
2003H		MVI C, COUNT
2005H	DELAY	DCR C
2006H		JNZ DELAY
2009H		MOV A, B
200AH		OUTPORT#
200CH		JMP NEXT

The C register is the time delay register which is loaded by a value COUNT to produce a time delay of 1ms.

To find the value of COUNT we do:
$T_D = T_L + T_O$
where,
T_D = Time Delay
T_L = Time delay inside loop
T_O = Time delay outside loop

The delay loop includes two instructions- DCR C (4 T-states) and JNZ (10 T-states).
So T_L = 14*Clock period*COUNT
=> 14*(0.5*10^{-6})*COUNT
=> (7*10^{-6})*COUNT

Delay outside the loop includes:

DCR B : 4T
MVI C, COUNT : 7T
MOV A, B : 4T

OUTPORT : 10T
JMP : 10T
Total : 35T
T_0= 35*Clock period => 17.5 microseconds
So, 1ms= (17.5+ 7*COUNT) microsecond
Therefore, COUNT= $(140)_{10}$

8085 program to convert an 8 bit BCD number into hexadecimal number

Problem

Write an assembly language program in 8085 microprocessor to convert an 8 bit BCD number into hexadecimal number.

Assumptions

Assume that starting address of the program is 2000, input memory locations, 2050, 2051, and output memory location is 2052.

Example

INPUT: 2050:02H
    2051: 09H

OUTPUT: 2052: 1DH

Algorithm

1.   Initialize memory pointer to 2050
2.   Get the most significant digit
3.   Multiply the MSD by 10 using repeated addition
4.   Add LSD to result obtained in above step
5.   Store the converted result in memory 2052

Program

Address	Mnemonics	Comment
2000	LXI H, 2050	
2003	MOV A, M	A<-M
2004	ADD A	A<-A+A
2005	MOV B, A	B<-A
2006	ADD A	A<-A+A
2007	ADD A	A
2008	ADD B	A<-A+B
2009	INX H	
200A	ADD M	A<-A+M
200B	INX H	
200C	MOV M, A	M<-A
200D	HLT	Terminate the Program

Explanation

Registers H, L, B, A are used for general purpose.

1. LXI H, 2050: will load the HL pair register with the address 2050 of memory location.
2. MOV A, M: copies the content of memory into register A.
3. ADD A: add the content of accumulator with itself.
4. MOV B, A: move the content of accumulator into register B.
5. ADD A: add the content of accumulator with itself.
6. ADD A: add the content of accumulator with itself.
7. ADD B: add the content of accumulator with register B and store the result in accumulator.

8. INX H: increment register pair HL.
9. ADD M: add the content of accumulator with memory and store the result in accumulator.
10. INX H: increment register pair HL.
11. MOV M, A: copies the content of accumulator into memory.
12. HLT: stops executing the program and halts any further execution.

8085 program to multiply two 16-bit numbers

Problem

Write an assembly language program in 8085 microprocessor to multiply two 16 bit numbers.

Assumption

- Starting address of program: 2000
- Input memory location: 2050, 2051, 2052, 2053
- Output memory location: 2054, 2055, 2056, 2057

Example

INPUT:
    (2050H) = 04H
    (2051H) = 07H
    (2052H) = 02H
    (2053H) = 01H
OUTPUT:
    (2054H) = 08H
    (2055H) = 12H
    (2056H) = 01H
    (2057H) = 0oH
RESULT:
Hence we have multiplied two 16 bit numbers.

Algorithm

Load the first data in HL pair.

1. Move content of HL pair to stack pointer.
2. Load the second data in HL pair and move it to DE.
3. Make H register as 00H and L register as 00H.
4. ADD HL pair and stack pointer.
5. Check for carry if carry increment it by 1 else move to next step.
6. Then move E to A and perform OR operation with accumulator and register D.
7. The value of operation is zero, then store the value else goto step 3.

Program

Address	Mnemonics	Comment
2000	LHLD 2050	Load H-L pair with address 2050
2003	SPHL	Save it in Stack Pointer
2004	LHLD 2052	Load H-L pair with address 2052
2007	XCHG	Exchange HL and DE Pair Content
2008	LXI H,0000H	H<-00H,L<-00H
200B	LXI B,0000H	B<-00H,C<-00H
200E	DAD SP	
200F	JNC 2013	Jump Not Carry
2012	INX B	Increment BC BY 1
2013	DCX D	Decrement DE BY 1
2014	MOV A,E	A<-E
2015	ORA D	Or the Content of Accumulator And D Register

2016	JNZ 200E	Jump Not Zero
2019	SHLD 2054	L<-2053,H<-2054
201C	MOV L,C	L<-C
201D	MOV H,B	B<H
201E	SHLD 2056	L<-2055,H<-2056
2021	HLT	Terminates the Program

Explanation

Registers B, C, D, E, H, L and accumulator are used for general purpose.

1. LHLD 2050: load HL pair with address 2050.
2. SPHL: save the content of HL in stack pointer.
3. LHLD 2052: load H-L pair with address 2052.
4. XCHG: exchange the content of HL pair with DE.
5. LXI H, 0000H: make H as 00H and L as 00H.
6. LXI B, 0000H: make B as 00h and C as 00H
7. DAD SP: ADD HL pair and stack pointer.
8. JNC 2013: jump to address 2013 if there will be no carry.
9. INX B: increments BC register with 1.
10. DCX D: decrements DE register pair by 1.
11. MOV A, E: move the content of register E to accumulator.
12. ORA D: or the content of accumulator and D register.
13. JNZ 200E: jump to address 200E if there will be no zero.
14. SHLD 2054: store the result to memory address 2054 and 2055 from HL pair register.
15. MOV L, C: move the content of register C to L.
16. MOV H, B: move the content of register B to H.
17. SHLD 2056: store the result to memory address 2056 and 2057 from HL pair register.
18. HLT: terminates the program.

8085 program to subtract two 16-bit numbers with or without borrow

Write an assembly language program in 8085 microprocessor to subtract two 16 bit numbers.

Assumption

- Starting address of program: 2000
- Input memory location: 2050, 2051, 2052, 2053
- Output memory location: 2054, 2055

Example
INPUT:

    (2050H) = 19H
    (2051H) = 6AH
    (2052H) = 15H
    (2053H) = 5CH

OUTPUT:

    (2054H) = 04H
    (2055H) = OEH

RESULT:
Hence we have subtracted two 16 bit numbers.

Algorithm

1. Get the LSB in L register and MSB in H register of 16 Bit number.
2. Exchange the content of HL register with DE register.
3. Again Get the LSB in L register and MSB in H register of 16 Bit number.
4. Subtract the content of L register from the content of E register.
5. Subtract the content of H register from the content of D register and borrow from previous step.
6. Store the result in memory location.

Program

Address	Mnemonics	Comment
2000	LHLD 2050	Load H-L pair with address 2050
2003	XCHG	Exchange H-L Pair with D-E Pair
2004	LHLD 2052	Load H-L pair with address 2052
2007	MVI C, 00	C<-00H
2009	MOV A, E	A<-E
200A	SUB L	A<-A-L
200B	STA 2054	2054<-A
200E	MOV A, D	A<-D
200F	SBB H	Subtract with Borrow
2010	STA 2055	2055<-A
2013	HLT	Terminates the Program

Explanation

1. LHLD 2050: load HL pair with address 2050.
2. XCHG: exchange the content of HL pair with DE.
3. LHLD 2052: load HL pair with address 2050.
4. MOV A, E: move the content of register E to A.
5. SUB L: subtract the content of A with the content of register L.
6. STA 2054: store the result from accumulator to memory address 2054.
7. MOV A, D: move the content of register D to A.

8. **SBB H:** subtract the content of A with the content of register H with borrow.
9. **STA 2055:** store the result from accumulator to memory address 2055.
10. **HLT:** stops executing the program and halts any further execution.

8085 program to find the range of bytes

Problem

Write an assembly language program that if an input number BYTE1 lies b/w 50H to 80H display it on output *PORT2*. If BYTE1 is less then 50H then simply print 00H at the output *PORT1*.

Examples

Input: 64H
Output: output at PORT2 -->64H
Input: 40H
Output: output at PORT1 -->00H

Algorithm

1. Load the BYTE1 in accumulator A.
2. Copy the Data from the accumulator to register B.
3. Subtract the 50H from the accumulator (BYTE).
4. Jump if subtraction is negative.
5. If jump condition is true then it will simply print 00H at PORT1.
6. If jump condition is false then BYTE1 will greater than 50H and in further instructions, it will also check the upper limit 80H of the BYTE1 so all the numbers lie b/w 50H to 80H those will print at PORT2.

Program

Address	Mnemonics	Comment
2000	MVI A, BYTE1	[A]<–[BYTE1]
2002	MOV B, A	[B]<–[A]

2003	SUI 50H	[A]<-[A-50]H
2004	JC DELETE	Jump to DELETE, if CY=1
2007	MOV A, B	[A]<-[B]
2008	SUI 80H	[A]<-[A-80]H
2009	JC DISPLAY	Jump to DISPLAY, if CY=1
200A	DELETE:XRA A	[A]<-[A Exclusive OR A]
200B	OUT PORT1	output the content of the accumulator at PORT1
200C	HLT	program termination
200D	DISPLAY:MOV A, B	[A]<-[B]
200E	OUT PORT2	output the content of the accumulator at PORT2
200F	HLT	program termination

Explanation

1. MVI A, BYTE1: load the accumulator A from BYTE1.
2. MOV B, A: copy the content of accumulator to register B.
3. SUI 50H: subtract the 50H from the content of the accumulator (BYTE1) and load it into accumulator.
4. JC DELETE: here JC is jump instruction with carry flag check condition, carry flag will 1 if the subtraction is negative if the subtraction is positive then carry flag will be 0. SUI 50H will be positive if Accumulator content (BYTE1) will be greater or equal to 50H. If CY=0 result is positive and no jump will be performed.
5. MOV A, B: copy the content of register B (BYTE1) to accumulator.
6. SUI 80H: subtract the 80H from the accumulator. If the accumulator content will be less than 80H then result will be positive and it will jump to DISPLAY label and display the BYTE at PORT2 if the number will be in range 50H to 7FH.
7. If in step-4, JC DELETE true means the subtraction result will positive then it will jump to delete and clear the content of accumulator and display 00H at output PORT1.

www.ingramcontent.com/pod-product-compliance
Lightning Source LLC
Chambersburg PA
CBHW031220050326
40689CB00009B/1409